# Introduction to Disciplined Agile Delivery

## A Small Agile Team's Journey from Scrum to Continuous Delivery

by Mark Lines and Scott W. Ambler

## Dedications

For Louise, Brian, and Katherine
- Mark

For Beverley and Olivia
- Scott

# CONTENTS

|  | Acknowledgments | 4 |
| 1 | Introduction | 5 |
| 2 | Reality over Rhetoric | 7 |
| 3 | Disciplined Agile Delivery in a Nutshell | 9 |
| 4 | Introduction to the Case Study | 27 |
| 5 | Inception | 31 |
| 6 | Construction Iteration C1 | 45 |
| 7 | Construction Iteration C2 | 53 |
| 8 | Construction Iteration C3 | 61 |
| 9 | Construction Iteration C7 | 67 |
| 10 | Construction Iteration C10 | 71 |
| 11 | Transition | 75 |
| 12 | Future Releases | 79 |
| 13 | Closing Thoughts | 87 |
|  | Appendix: The Disciplined Agile IT Department | 89 |

## Acknowledgements

We'd like to thank Beverley Ambler, Rod Bray, David Dame, Louise Lines, Glen Little, Valentin-Tudor Mocanu, Kristen Morton, David Shapiro, Paul Sims, and Michael Vizdos for their feedback and input into the development of this book. We couldn't have done it without you.

Illustrations and cover design by Nicole Wolf
Cry Wolf Illustration (crywolfillustration@gmail.com)

# 1 INTRODUCTION

Many organizations are struggling to be successful with mainstream agile methods such as Scrum. Sometimes the impulse is to give up and try the *next great thing* such as Lean or Scaled Agile Framework (SAFe). The reality is that the source of failure of existing agile adoptions can often be traced to either the misapplication of core agile principles or a naïve approach to scaling agile and the need to address enterprise concerns.

Adding to the confusion is the constant bickering in the agile community about what method is best between Scrum, XP, Kanban, SAFe and others. The reality is that most organizations can benefit from a number of these strategies, albeit with some consistency that a common framework can provide. This is where Disciplined Agile Delivery (DAD) comes in.

DAD is a hybrid of existing methods that provides the flexibility to use various approaches as well as plugging some gaps not addressed by mainstream agile methods. In a nutshell, DAD is "pragmatic agile." It describes proven strategies to adapt and scale your agile initiatives to suit the unique realities of your enterprise without having to figure it all out by yourself.

The book "Disciplined Agile Delivery: A Practitioner's Guide to Software Development in the Enterprise" is the definitive guide for DAD. However, DAD continues to evolve so the most recent material can be found on the DAD Blog at DisciplinedAgileDelivery.com

While the book on DAD is quite comprehensive in describing the framework, it is 500 pages. We felt that it would be useful to summarize DAD into a quick read to show how it can be applied in a typical situation. We have found that organizations that simply take a bit of time to understand what DAD is, as well as what it is not, see very quickly the obvious benefits of the DAD framework.

We wrote this short book in the hope that after having invested just an hour or two to learn about what DAD actually is, you are convinced that it is worthwhile to further investigate the possible fit for DAD within your organization.

Some quick facts about the DAD framework:

* DAD is resonating within organizations around the world.

Organizations that have adopted, or are in the process of adopting the DAD framework include large financial institutions, software companies, e-commerce companies, restaurant chains, government agencies, and many others. By adoption, we mean either planning or actively implementing it across their entire organization, not just in one or two teams.

- Although DAD was originally developed at IBM, it is now the intellectual property of the Disciplined Agile Consortium, and is freely available for use.
    - o The certification program is described at DisciplinedAgileConsortium.org
- DAD is not a replacement for existing agile and lean methods. It complements them and in many cases extends them to be enterprise ready.

# 2 REALITY OVER RHETORIC

One of the reasons why DAD is quickly growing in popularity is that it acknowledges the realities of how organizations that are effectively scaling agile are *really* doing things. We think that it is important to clear up some of the misconceptions regarding the hype of agile purism versus what we have found to be really going on based on both our hands-on experience at many clients around the world and our comprehensive industry research[1].

| Myth | Reality |
|---|---|
| **Agile teams don't do requirements or planning** | The average agile team spends about one month doing some upfront planning and requirements modeling. While DAD seeks to minimize this work, we acknowledge this reality and suggest that teams new to agile spend a few weeks in an Inception phase to complete the work in a minimal yet sufficient fashion. |
| **DAD is a form of "WaterScrumFall" with lots of upfront planning and requirements (Water), and testing and deployment at the end (Fall), with Scrum in the middle** | While DAD acknowledges that some pre-work is required to secure funding, amongst other pre-coding activities, DAD stresses to minimize the work in Inception. Similarly, while DAD recognizes that the common pattern in enterprises is to deploy solutions in a structured fashion, which we describe as the Transition phase, the disciplined testing practices in the Construction phase – such as continuous integration – should minimize the transition effort and end of lifecycle testing. For more advanced applications of DAD, the teams may not even require an explicit |

---

[1] See ScottAmbler.com/insights.html & Ambysoft.com/surveys/

| | |
|---|---|
| | Inception or Transition phase as described in the Continuous Delivery DAD lifecycle. |
| **"Governance" is an agile dirty word. The agile concept of self-organization means that enterprises should not interfere with how agile teams deliver their software.** | Governance is actually a good thing when it's done in an agile/lean manner. Sponsors and the enterprise as a whole deserve to know that their investments are being properly spent and that the risk of project delivery is monitored and controlled, albeit in a lightweight agile fashion. DAD provides specific guidance to fulfill this responsibility in a relatively painless fashion. |
| **DAD is complicated and would be disruptive to adopt.** | DAD is quite simple to adopt especially if your organization is familiar with common agile practices. The good news is that DAD provides guidance that addresses why some existing agile implementations are struggling and can help to bring these implementations back on track. |
| **SAFe is THE solution to scaling agile** | For large organizations that have project teams greater than 100 people, SAFe may indeed be a good fit for *some* projects. However, most organizations have a mix of small to medium-sized teams delivering solutions for multiple lines of business. In these situations SAFe may not be suitable. While SAFe is suitable in a specific context, DAD is much more flexible and adaptable to a broader range of situations in the enterprise. |

# 3 DISCIPLINED AGILE DELIVERY IN A NUTSHELL

## Key Points

- DAD is a process decision framework, not just another methodology
- If you are using Scrum, XP, Kanban, or SAFe, you are already using variations and a subset of the DAD framework
- DAD provides four lifecycles to choose from, it doesn't prescribe a single way of working – choice is good
- DAD focuses on achieving common goals in an agile manner, not the production of specific work products nor on following a prescriptive agile strategy
- DAD addresses key enterprise concerns not described by mainstream methods such as Scrum
- DAD is complementary to SAFe yet less prescriptive and more practical for most enterprises
- DAD shows how agile works from end-to-end
- DAD provides a flexible foundation from which to scale mainstream methods
- While DAD's philosophy is consistent with that of the Agile Manifesto, it includes additional guidance to be effective in more complex enterprise situations[2]
- It is *not* difficult to get started with DAD

## What is DAD?

Many organizations start their agile journey by adopting Scrum because it describes a good strategy for leading agile software teams. However, Scrum is only a small part of what is required to

---

[2] See Disciplinedagiledelivery.com/disciplinedagilemanifesto/ for an enterprise extension to the Agile Manifesto

deliver sophisticated solutions to your stakeholders. Invariably, teams need to look to other methods to fill in the process gaps that Scrum purposely ignores. When looking at other methods, there is considerable overlap and conflicting terminology that can be confusing to practitioners as well as outside stakeholders. Worse yet, people don't always know where to look for advice or even know what issues they need to consider.

To address these challenges, the Disciplined Agile Delivery (DAD) process decision framework provides a more cohesive approach to agile solution delivery. To be more exact, here's a definition: "The Disciplined Agile Delivery (DAD) process decision framework is a people-first, learning-oriented, hybrid agile approach to IT solution delivery. It has a risk-value delivery lifecycle, is goal-driven, enterprise aware, and scalable."

There are clearly some interesting aspects to the DAD framework. DAD is a hybrid approach that extends Scrum with proven strategies from Agile Modeling (AM), Extreme Programming (XP), Unified Process (UP), Kanban, Lean Software Development, Outside In Development (OID) and several other methods. DAD is a non-proprietary, freely available framework. DAD extends the construction-focused lifecycle of Scrum to address the full, end-to-end delivery lifecycle from project initiation all the way to delivering the solution to its end users. It also supports lean and continuous delivery versions of the lifecycle: unlike other agile methods, DAD doesn't prescribe a single lifecycle because it recognizes that one process size does not fit all. DAD includes advice about the technical practices such as those from Extreme Programming (XP) as well as the modeling, documentation, and governance strategies missing from both Scrum and XP. Instead of the prescriptive approach seen in other agile methods, including Scrum, the DAD framework takes a goals-driven approach. In doing so, DAD provides contextual advice regarding viable alternatives and their trade-offs, enabling you to tailor DAD to effectively address the situation in which you find yourself. By describing what works, what doesn't work, and more importantly why, DAD helps you to increase your chance of adopting strategies that will work for you.

## People First: Roles in Disciplined Agile Delivery

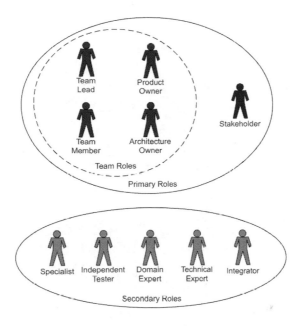

The DAD framework suggests a robust set of roles[3] for agile solution delivery. A common question that we get is what is the difference between primary and secondary roles? Primary roles exist in all DAD projects regardless of scale. Secondary roles, however, typically occur only at scale and sometimes only for a temporary period of time. Another common question that we get is "Why are there so many roles?" Scrum has three roles – ScrumMaster, Product Owner and Team Member – so why does DAD need ten? The primary issue is one of scope. Scrum mostly focuses on leadership and change management aspects during Construction and therefore has roles that reflect this. DAD on the other hand explicitly focuses on the entire delivery lifecycle and all aspects of solution delivery, including the technical aspects that Scrum leaves out. So, with a larger scope comes more roles. For example, because DAD encompasses **agile architecture** issues it

---

[3] For a detailed description of the DAD roles, see DisciplinedAgileDelivery.com/roles-on-dad-teams/

includes an Architecture Owner role. Scrum doesn't address architecture so it doesn't include this role.

## A Hybrid Framework

Disciplined Agile Delivery (DAD) is a hybrid framework that builds upon the solid foundation of other methods and software process frameworks. The DAD framework adopts practices and strategies from existing sources and provides advice for when and how to apply them together. In one sense, methods such as Scrum, Extreme Programming (XP), Kanban, and Agile Modeling (AM) provide the process bricks and DAD the mortar to fit the bricks together effectively.

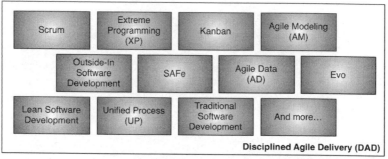

**Disciplined Agile Delivery (DAD)**

Copyright 2014 Disciplined Agile Consortium

One of the great advantages of agile and lean software development is the wealth of practices, techniques and strategies available to you. This is also one of its greatest challenges because without something like the DAD framework, it's difficult to know what to choose and how to fit them together. Worse yet, many teams new to agile will a method like Scrum or SAFe as if it's a recipe, ignoring advice from other sources and thereby getting into trouble.

## A Full Delivery Lifecycle

The focus of DAD is on delivery, although how other aspects of the system lifecycle affect the delivery lifecycle are also addressed. A full system/product lifecycle goes from the initial concept for the product, through delivery, to operations and support and often includes many iterations of the delivery lifecycle. The following diagram is a high-level view of the DAD lifecycle. The inner three phases – Inception, Construction, and Transition – form the delivery portion of the lifecycle. During this portion you incrementally build a consumable solution over time.

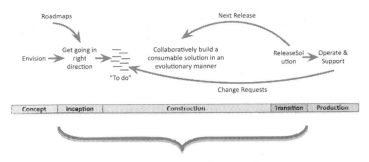

## The Delivery Lifecycle

Obviously there's more to DAD than what the high-level diagram shows. DAD, because it's not prescriptive and strives to reflect reality as best it can, supports several versions of a delivery lifecycle. Four versions of the lifecycle follow: an agile/basic version that extends the Scrum Construction lifecycle with proven ideas from RUP; an advanced/lean lifecycle; a continuous delivery lifecycle; and an exploratory lifecycle based upon a Lean Start-up approach. DAD teams will adopt a lifecycle that is most appropriate for their situation and then tailor it appropriately. For the purposes of this short DAD overview, we will not explain each of these lifecycles[4].

---

[4] Read DisciplinedAgileDelivery.com/lifecycle/ for details.

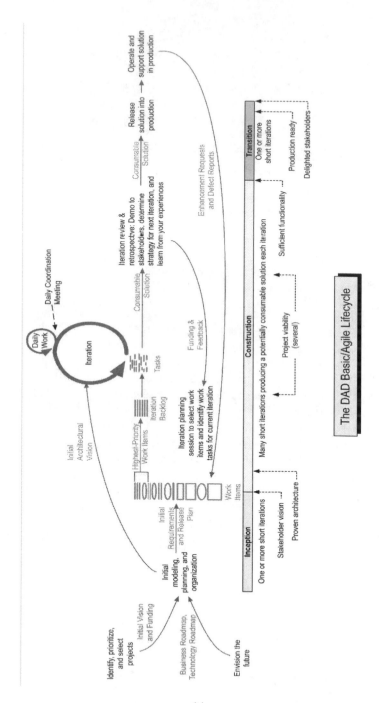

The DAD Basic/Agile Lifecycle

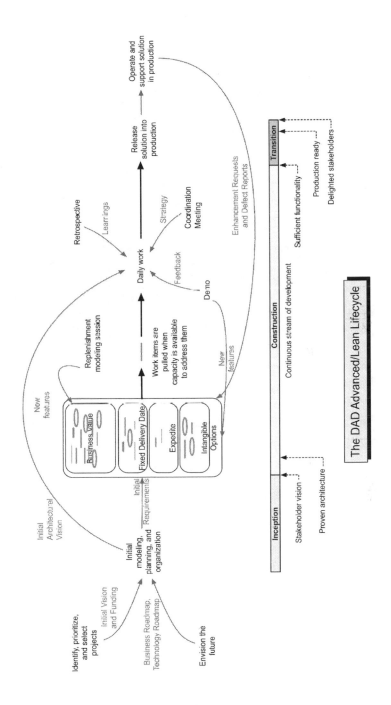

The DAD Advanced/Lean Lifecycle

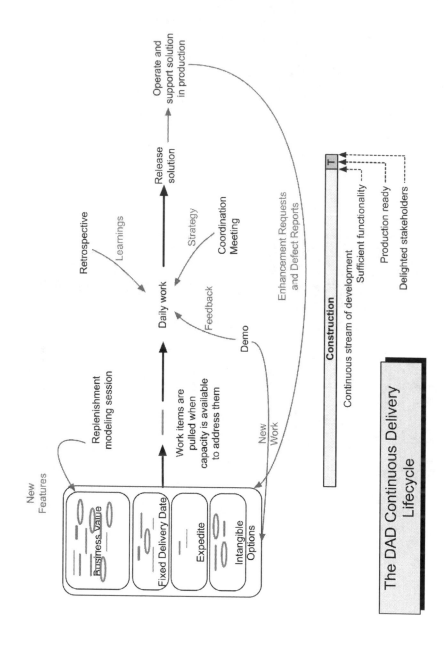

The DAD Continuous Delivery Lifecycle

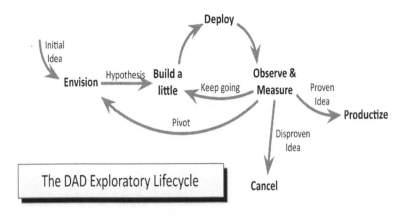

The DAD Exploratory Lifecycle

In general, we suggest the following guidance regarding which lifecycles fit in certain circumstances:

**Agile/Basic DAD Lifecycle.** This lifecycle is based largely upon Scrum and XP with a set of time boxed iterations (sprints) being the core of the Construction phase. It is the most commonly used lifecycle suitable in these types of situations:

- The work is primarily enhancements or new features
- The work can be identified, prioritized, and estimated early in the project
- A good choice for new agile teams
- The team is familiar with Scrum and XP

**Lean/Advanced DAD Lifecycle.** This lifecycle promotes lean principles such as minimizing work in process, maximizing flow, a continuous stream of work (instead of fixed iterations), and reducing bottlenecks. New work is pulled from the work item pool when the team has capacity. While Scrum prescribes the use of a set of "ceremonies", such as the daily co-ordination meeting (Scrum), iteration (sprint) planning sessions, retrospectives to be done on certain cadences within the iterations (sprints), Lean does not prescribe this overhead and instead suggests that it be done if and when necessary. This requires a degree of discipline and self-awareness not usually found on teams new to agile, hence this lifecycle is considered advanced. While the concepts of Lean and the Kanban system it uses are very easy to learn, it can be difficult to master the principles of lean flow and maximizing the throughput of the system. It is suitable in these situations:

- Work can be broken down into very small work items of roughly the same size
- Work is difficult to predict in advance. Projects that are focused on fixing defects or handling support issues are good candidates for this lifecycle
- The team favors the lean approach of minimizing batch size (which helps to reduce work in progress) and any planning in advance of doing the work.

**Continuous Delivery DAD Lifecycle.** This lifecycle is a natural progression from the Advanced/Lean lifecycle. It supports the goal of delivering increments of the solution in a more frequent manner than the other lifecycles. It requires a mature set of practices around continuous integration and deployment in order to be practical. It also requires the technical infrastructure and advanced DevOps practices that support this approach. It is best suited in these types of situations:

- Projects/solutions that can be delivered to stakeholders in a frequent and incremental basis
- Organizations with streamlined deployment practices and procedures
- Projects where getting value into the hands of stakeholders rapidly, before the entire solution is complete, is critical
- Teams with mature DevOps practices in place including; continuous integration, continuous deployment, and automated regression testing

**Exploratory Lifecycle.** This lifecycle is based on the Lean Start-up principles advocated by Eric Reis in his best-selling book, *The Lean Startup*. The philosophy is to minimize upfront investments in solutions in favor of small experiments that are market tested and measured early and often during the project. As the solution is being developed, the delivery team has the opportunity to deliver what is truly required based on feedback from actual usage. It is useful in these types of situations:

- The solution addresses a new unexplored market
- The stakeholders and delivery team are very flexible in adapting the solution as it is being developed
- You have a valid hypothesis/strategy to test with clear go/no-go criteria for when the test is over

## Disciplined Agile Teams are Goal-Driven

DAD's goal-driven approach enables DAD teams to avoid being prescriptive and thereby be more flexible and easier to scale than other agile methods. For example, where Scrum prescribes a value-driven Product Backlog approach to managing requirements, DAD instead says that during construction you have the goal of addressing changing stakeholder needs. DAD then indicates that there are several issues surrounding that goal that you need to consider, and there are several techniques/practices that you should consider adopting to do so. DAD goes further and describes the advantages and disadvantages of each technique and in what situations it is best suited. Yes, Scrum's Product Backlog approach is one way to address changing stakeholder needs but it isn't the only option nor is it the best option in many situations.

In the first DAD book[5], we described goals in a non-visual manner using tables that explored the advantages and disadvantages of the techniques associated with an issue. In the second half of 2012 we began expanding on this approach and developed a way to represent goals in a visual manner using what we call a process goal diagram[6]

Let's work through an example. The following figure depicts the goal diagram for *Explore Initial Scope*, a goal that you should address at the beginning of a project during the Inception phase (remember, DAD promotes a full delivery lifecycle, not just a construction lifecycle). Where some agile methods will simply advise you to populate your product backlog with some initial user stories, the goal diagram makes it clear that you might want to be a bit more sophisticated in your approach. What level of detail should you capture, if any (a light specification approach of writing up some index cards and a few whiteboard sketches is just one option you should consider)? What view types should you consider (user stories are one approach to usage modeling, but

---

[5] *Disciplined Agile Delivery: A Practitioner's Guide to Agile Software Delivery in the Enterprise* (Ambler and Lines, 2012).
6 All the process diagrams can be found at DisciplinedAgileDelivery.com/process-goals/

shouldn't you consider other views to explore the data or the UI)? Default techniques, or perhaps more accurately suggested starting points, are shown in bold italics. Notice how we suggest that you likely want to default to capturing usage in some way, basic domain concepts (for example, via a high-level conceptual diagram) in some way, and non-functional requirements in some way. There are different strategies you may want to consider for modeling.

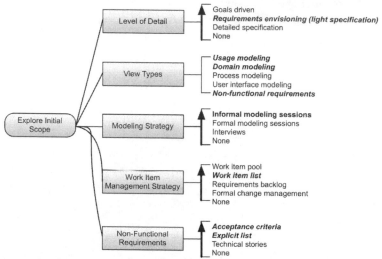

You should also start thinking about your approach to managing your work. In DAD, we make it clear that agile teams do more than just implement new requirements, hence our recommendation to default to a work item list over Scrum's simplistic Requirements Backlog strategy. Work items may include new requirements to be implemented, defects to be fixed, training workshops, reviews of other teams' work, and so on. These are all things that need to be sized, prioritized, and planned for. Finally, the goal diagram makes it clear that when you're exploring the initial scope of your effort that you should capture non-functional requirements – such as reliability, availability, and security requirements (among many) – in some manner.

There are several fundamental advantages to taking a goal-driven approach to agile solution delivery. First, a goal-driven approach supports process tailoring by making process decisions explicit. Second, it enables effective scaling by guiding you through tailoring your strategy to reflect the realities of the scaling factors which you face. Third, it makes your process options very clear and thereby makes it easier to identify the appropriate strategy for the situation you find yourself in. Fourth, it takes the guesswork out of extending agile methods and thereby enables you to focus on your actual job, which is to provide value to your stakeholders. Fifth, it makes it clear what risks you're taking on and thus enables you to increase the likelihood of project success. Sixth, and this may not be a benefit, it hints at an agile maturity model.

The mind map on the next page summarizes the goals for a DAD project grouped by the three phases of Inception, Construction, and Transition, as well as the goals that are ongoing throughout the project.

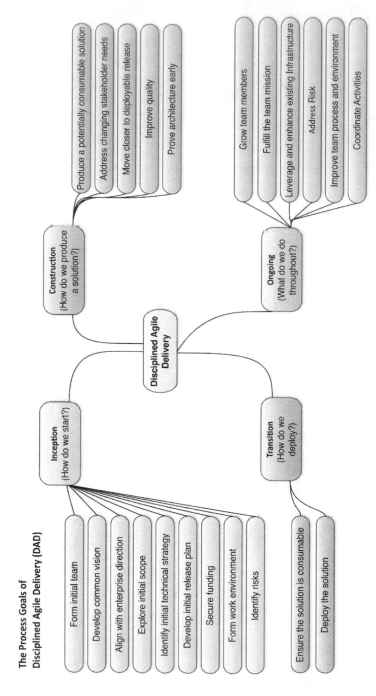

**The Process Goals of
Disciplined Agile Delivery (DAD)**

**Disciplined Agile Delivery**

**Inception**
(How do we start?)
- Form initial team
- Develop common vision
- Align with enterprise direction
- Explore initial scope
- Identify initial technical strategy
- Develop initial release plan
- Secure funding
- Form work environment
- Identify risks

**Construction**
(How do we produce a solution?)
- Produce a potentially consumable solution
- Address changing stakeholder needs
- Move closer to deployable release
- Improve quality
- Prove architecture early

**Transition**
(How do we deploy?)
- Ensure the solution is consumable
- Deploy the solution

**Ongoing**
(What do we do throughout?)
- Grow team members
- Fulfill the team mission
- Leverage and enhance existing Infrastructure
- Address Risk
- Improve team process and environment
- Coordinate Activities

## Disciplined Agile Teams are Enterprise Aware

Enterprise awareness is one of the key aspects of the Disciplined Agile Delivery (DAD) framework. The observation is that DAD teams work within your organization's enterprise ecosystem, as do all other teams. There are often existing systems currently in production and minimally, your solution shouldn't impact them. Better yet, your solution will hopefully leverage existing functionality and data available in production. You will often have other teams working in parallel with your team and you may wish to take advantage of a portion of what they're doing and vice versa. Your organization may be working towards business or technical visions to which your team should contribute. A governance strategy exists which hopefully enhances what your team is doing.

Enterprise awareness is an important aspect of self discipline because as a professional you should strive to do what's right for your organization and not just what's interesting to you. Teams developing in isolation may choose to build something from scratch, or use different development tools, or create different data sources, when perfectly good ones that have been successfully installed, tested, configured, and fine-tuned already exist within the organization. Disciplined agile professionals will:

- Work closely with enterprise professionals, such as enterprise architects and portfolio managers
- Adopt and follow enterprise guidance
- Leverage enterprise assets, including existing systems and data sources
- Enhance your organizational ecosystem via refactoring enterprise assets
- Adopt a DevOps culture
- Share learnings and knowledge with other teams
- Adopt appropriate governance strategies, including open and honest monitoring

Enterprise awareness is important for several reasons. First, you can reduce overall delivery time and cost by leveraging existing assets. In other words, DAD teams can spend less time reinventing the wheel and more time producing real value for their stakeholders. Second, by working closely with enterprise professionals, DAD teams can get going in the right direction

23

easily. Third, it increases the chance that your delivery team will help to optimize the organizational whole, and not just the "solution part" that it is tasked to work on. As the lean software development movement aptly shows, this increases team effectiveness by reducing time to market.

## DAD Provides The Foundation for Scaling Agile

When he was with IBM Rational, Scott led the development effort of the basic strategy represented in the following figure. The fundamental observation was that many organizations were struggling with how to scale agile methods, in particular Scrum. We felt that the first step was to identify how to successfully develop a solution from end-to-end. Although mainstream agile methods clearly provided many great strategies, there really wasn't any sort of glue beyond consultantware (i.e. "Hire me and I'll show you how to do it") putting it all together. This is where the DAD framework comes in, but that's only a start as you also need to tailor your approach to reflect the context in which you find yourself.

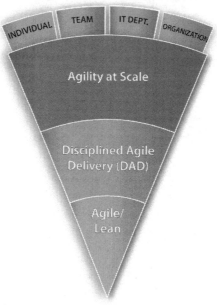

The DAD framework provides a better foundation for scaling agile in several ways. First, it promotes a risk-value lifecycle - attacking the riskier work early in an endeavor in order to help eliminate some or all of the risk, thereby increasing the chance of project success. Some people like to refer to this as an aspect of "failing fast" although we like to put it in terms of succeeding early. Second, DAD promotes self organization enhanced with effective governance based on the observation that agile project teams work within the scope and constraints of a larger, organizational ecosystem. As a result, DAD recommends that you adopt an effective governance strategy that guides and enables agile teams. Third, DAD promotes the delivery of consumable solutions over just the construction of working software. In addition to producing software, DAD teams also create supporting documentation, they need to upgrade and/or redeploy the hardware the software runs on, they potentially change the business process around the usage of the system, and may even motivate changes to the organization structure of the people using the system. Fourth, as described earlier, DAD promotes enterprise awareness over team awareness. Fifth, DAD is context-sensitive and goal driven, not prescriptive. One process size does not fit all, and effective teams tailor their strategy to reflect the situation in which they find themselves.

Now let's examine what it means to scale agile. When many people hear "scaling" they often think about large teams that may be geographically distributed in some way. This clearly happens, and people are clearly succeeding at applying agile in these sorts of situations, but there's often more to scaling than this. Organizations are also applying agile in compliance situations, either regulatory compliance that is imposed upon them or self-selected compliance (such as CMMI and ISO). They are also applying agile to a range of problem and solution complexities, and even when multiple organizations are involved (as in outsourcing). The following figure summarizes the potential scaling factors that you need to consider when tailoring your agile strategy.

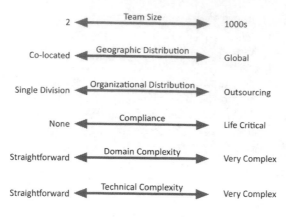

## In Summary

The Disciplined Agile Delivery (DAD) process decision framework provides a pragmatic approach from which to scale agile strategies to address the unique situations in which teams find themselves. DAD explicitly addresses the issues faced by enterprise agile teams that many agile methodologies prefer to gloss over. This includes how to successfully initiate agile teams in a streamlined manner, how architecture fits into the agile lifecycle, how to address documentation effectively, how to address quality issues in an enterprise environment, how agile analysis techniques are applied to address the myriad of stakeholder concerns, and many more.

# 4 INTRODUCTION TO THE CASE STUDY

We are now going to describe what you might expect on a typical DAD project using a fictitious case study based on a retail bank called "BigBank." The company would like to start a project to enable prospective customers to apply for a mortgage on-line. The solution should be easy to use on both a desktop browser as well as mobile responsive devices.

After trying Scrum on several project teams, BigBank realized that they needed to adopt an agile method that reflected the enterprise challenges they faced. In the words of one of their senior developers "Scrum leaves us hanging on too many things, and my team doesn't have the time to figure out all the stuff that Scrum doesn't address." After a bit of investigation they chose to adopt the DAD framework because it offered the flexibility that they required. BigBank liked the fact that DAD includes a lifecycle that extends and enhances Scrum's lifecycle, allowing them to retain the investment that they've made in Scrum. Given DAD's lack of prescription and focus on pragmatism, BigBank recognized that DAD would scale to meet its diverse needs.

As described previously, DAD is a process decision framework that provides guidance for the hundreds of decisions made on a typical project. For the purposes of this case study, we will only discuss a small number of decisions with the intent of illustrating how DAD can serve as a lightweight framework that provides guidance for the entire delivery lifecycle. Admittedly, in the interest of brevity this is an oversimplification of a typical project.

## The Team

Let's introduce the team.

 **Patricia** the **Product Owner (PO)**: Patricia works for Berhard, the primary business sponsor. She has no technical background but has been asked to be the Product Owner for this project. She is stressed about having to work full time in the same work area as the rest of the development team.

**Barbara the Business Analyst (BA)**: Barbara is a consultant who brings many years of experience with modeling and elicitation of requirements and business process design. She reports to Patricia.

 **Terry** the **Team Lead**: Terry was previously a Certified ScrumMaster (CSM) but recently took a DAD workshop which opened his eyes to responsibilities in an enterprise situation that extend beyond just those of ScrumMaster. As such, he took it upon himself to lead the rest of the team on DAD during this pilot project.

 **Carlos the Coach:** Carlos is a Green Belt certified DAD coach and draws upon his years of experience seeing patterns of both success and failure on agile projects. He is coaching several DAD teams besides this one.

 **Ashok** the **Architecture Owner (AO)**: Although Ashok is definitely a senior developer he realizes that being an Architecture Owner includes responsibilities beyond being the smartest and most experienced developer on the team.

 **Danny** the **Developer**: Danny is a junior developer who has been with BigBank for two years. Danny is very excited to be on an agile team.

 **Debbie** the **Developer:** Debbie is an intermediate developer who has worked on web-based systems her entire career. She isn't sure about this new agile approach, but is willing to give it a try.

 **Tara** the **Tester:** This is Tara's first agile project. She has always applied traditional testing practices on previous projects.

**Dick** the **Database Administrator:** Dick has always worked on projects that do complete requirements and design at the beginning of the project. He expects that the database logical and physical designs will be completed and reviewed by his group before any coding begins. Terry has explained to him that he will need to take an evolutionary approach for the agile project which he is not too happy about. Although Dick is only available to the team 25% of the time, it is his highest priority.

Now let's introduce the primary stakeholders:

 **Victoria** the **VP of IT:** Victoria has asked this project to pilot the DAD approach and is interested to know how it can help deliver the promise of agile that they have not been seeing from their adoption of Scrum.

 **Berhard** the **Business Stakeholder and Sponsor:** Although Berhard is sponsoring this project he has many other responsibilities.

 **Chris** the **Certified ScrumMaster (CSM):** Chris is *not part of the team* but is an interested observer. He takes a "no compromise" approach to Scrum and is not sure why we would need DAD in addition to Scrum.

 **Enrico** the **Enterprise Architect:** Enrico is responsible for ensuring that all IT solutions are well designed and can support non-functional requirements such as security, scalability, and fault tolerance. He is worried about agile teams ignoring standards and existing assets such as proven services that are available for reuse.

 **Oliver** the **Operations Manager:** Oliver and his team will have to deploy and support this application when it goes into Production.

**Samira** the **Support Supervisor**: Samira manages the support center and is concerned about how issues will be resolved by the team after it is deployed into Production.

 **Mindy** the **VP of Marketing**: Mindy's team is responsible for all public-facing messaging for BigBank. Her team will need to put the marketing program together for this new customer offering.

 **Padma** the **PMO Lead**: Padma is responsible for reporting the health of all projects and assessing delivery risk across the project portfolio.

## The Approach

One of the very first decisions that any team needs to make is which of DAD's four lifecycles to use for this project. Based on a suggestion from Terry the Team Lead, the team elected to use the Scrum-based Agile/Basic DAD lifecycle for the following reasons:

- The team is new to agile, and the basic lifecycle provides sufficient structure for new teams
- The work can be identified, prioritized, and estimated (at a high-level) in advance, although requirements are still expected to evolve over time

We pick up this case study at the beginning of the Inception phase.

# 5 INCEPTION

The Inception phase in DAD is an explicit team initiation effort. It should be as lightweight and short as possible. You want to form your team and perform sufficient modeling and planning so that you can get going in the right direction. You do this at a high level to think through the major issues that you will face, trusting that your team will be able to handle the details as they evolve.

**Team Kick-off Meeting:** Terry schedules a meeting with the team for a team kickoff. They gather Monday morning. Terry asks Berhard, who is the sponsor, to kick-off the meeting by explaining the need for the new Mortgage Application Portal (MAP) and how it is a critical business initiative to attract new mortgage customers to the bank. After Berhard answers several questions from the team, Terry describes the strategy for developing the MAP solution using the DAD framework. He explains to the team that he has time-boxed three weeks for the Inception phase. While he expects that future releases of the solution will require shorter Inception phases he feels that it is prudent to start with a longer Inception because the team is new to DAD and training will be part of this phase. The purpose/milestone for this phase is to obtain agreement that the vision for the project makes sense from the perspective of all stakeholders. He explains that this means that they need to do "just enough" work to define things that you might find in a typical project charter, albeit in a lightweight fashion. Using a projector, Terry reviews the nine Inception goals for DAD's Inception phase.

**Inception Goals**

- Form initial team
- Develop common vision
- Align with enterprise direction
- Explore initial scope
- Identify initial technical strategy
- Develop initial release plan
- Secure funding
- Form work environment
- Identify risks

**Terry:** Looks like we are well on the way to achieving these goals. We already have formed the initial team. As part of developing a common vision we will work on the other goals shown here in parallel. Let's discuss our strategy for the next three weeks to gather information necessary to achieve these goals:

- **Align with Enterprise Direction**: Terry asks Ashok to schedule a meeting with Enrico to obtain information on any existing architecture assets, patterns, standards and guidelines that the team should be aware of. He suggests that Enrico share information on the enterprise architectural vision so that the new solution is aligned properly.

- **Explore Initial Scope**: Patricia plans to schedule meetings with business stakeholders (Berhard and several others) to build a prioritized backlog of agile requirements (stories). Barbara the BA will assist Patricia with facilitation of these meetings.

- **Identify Initial Technical Strategy**: Ashok will spend some time with Terry and the other developers to model an initial architectural strategy using some lightweight modeling techniques.

- **Develop Initial Release Plan**: Once the Initial Scope has been determined, Terry will ask that Patricia schedule a meeting to do estimation with the team so that a high-level release plan can be determined.

- **Secure Funding**: Berhard has already decided to fund the three-week Inception phase and has tentatively set aside funding for the next four months for the Construction and Transition phases. He understands that the funding level may need to be negotiated based on the findings during Inception.

- **Form Work Environment**: While the team is currently scattered across three floors of the building, Terry wants to move the team to a common work area. He plans to work with the facilities team to establish a new work space.

- **Identify Risks**: Terry asks Ashok to work with him on creating a list of risks with mitigation strategies. Many of these risks are expected to be technical in nature depending on the technical strategy selected as well as the non-functional requirements that will be flushed out as part of exploring the initial scope.

## Week One of Inception

To ensure that everyone is on the same page and is familiar both with agile fundamentals as well as the DAD framework, the team attends a 3-day *DA101 Disciplined Agile Delivery Experience* workshop[7]. On Thursday they jump in and start a series of workshops to do the work required to meet the Inception milestone of attaining stakeholder agreement on the solution vision. For most of these meetings the core team will participate along with other interested stakeholders depending on the type of workshop. Carlos will attend the meetings to help facilitate the workshops. Coaching a team is particularly useful following a workshop to engrain the concepts learned.

**Patricia works on identifying the initial scope.** Patricia meets with the business stakeholders to start work on identifying the initial scope. Referring to the *Explore Initial Scope* goal diagram from DAD, the team decides to do some usage modeling to flush out the high-level requirements. The diagram suggests that this type of modeling is a good strategy to use on your initial DAD projects. They choose to use a Story Map[8] to organize the system flows into high-level epics and stories, each of which is written on a separate index card. The epics are written on orange cards and the stories on yellow. On the backs of the cards are a set of high-level acceptance criteria that describe what conditions need to be met for the story on each card to be considered complete by Patricia (the product owner). Many of the stories will be too big to implement in a single iteration and will need to be broken down into smaller stories but at this point they are sufficient for conveying the high-level initial scope.

---

[7] DAD course offerings can be found at DisciplinedAgileConsortium.org
[8] See *User Story Mapping* by Jeff Patton, O'Reilly Media 2014.

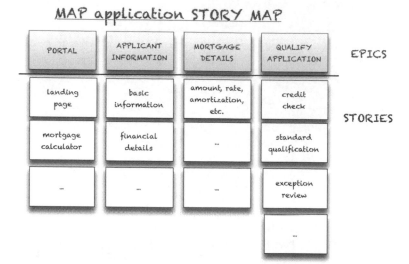

**Ashok leads the team in identifying the initial technical strategy.** Terry and the developers meet amongst themselves to evaluate potential architectural strategies for this solution. They refer to BigBank's technical roadmap, enterprise standards, and reference architecture documentation to see if there are existing assets such as templates, services/APIs, and data sources that they can reuse. As suggested by DAD's *Identify Initial Technical Strategy* goal, they choose to keep the level of detail at a high level, gather their ideas via informal modeling sessions and focus on a single candidate architecture. The architecture envisioning workshop takes a full day. The team is able to find a large meeting room to do this work that has a large table and a lot of wall space. Unfortunately there was only one small whiteboard at the front of the room. Terry orders several rolls of "whiteboard wallpaper" that attaches to the wall via static cling. After taking down several framed motivational pictures, they use the wallpaper to turn the side walls into workable whiteboards.

Terry conveys to the team that Enrico mentioned that the Enterprise Architecture (EA) group wants to move away from the current monolithic architecture to a micro-services model over time. They would also like to use "feature toggles" to be able to share all code on one mainline branch rather than working in separate feature branches, controlling what is actually deployed using these toggles. This will provide isolation of deployed functionality so that there is no single source of failure that could bring the whole system down. This will reduce deployment risk in the future and facilitate smaller deployments on a much more frequent basis.

BigBank's technology roadmap, created by the enterprise architecture team, defines this strategy. New functionality will be built along the micro-services/feature toggle strategy. Existing legacy code and data sources will be refactored over time on an as-needed basis[9].

During the architecture envisioning workshop Dick brings up the need to create a comprehensive data model before Construction can begin. Carlos points out that with an agile approach the detailed design emerges over the course of development. At this point in time the team only needs to invest enough modeling effort to get going in the right direction. The team has done enough requirements and architecture modeling to drive the planning efforts that will occur

---

[9] For practical strategies, see *Working Effectively with Legacy Code* by Michael Feathers (Prentice Hall 2004) and *Refactoring Databases* by Scott Ambler and Pramod Sadalage (Addison Wesley 2006).

next week. Dick is clearly not comfortable with this strategy, but agrees to wait and see how well it works in practice.

One of the things that the Mortgage Application Portal (MAP) must be able to do is determine whether someone is an existing BigBank customer. Ashok points out that BigBank's technology roadmap calls out a collection of reusable web services that will do that and more. These web services are currently under development and that basic customer information access services should be available two months from now. These services are being developed by "Team X-Ray" following a traditional waterfall style of approach. Dick says that it would be easier to just write simple SQL statements in their code to access the required legacy data. Ashok agrees that would be an easier approach, but that it would only be a short-term solution that would increase overall technical debt within BigBank because yet another application would be directly coupled to the legacy data sources. Carlos suggests that the team should work in a more disciplined, enterprise-aware manner that reflects the overall strategy of BigBank. A bit of extra work now will result in a more robust solution, although it increases the risk that the team faces as they now depend on Team X-Ray to deliver the required web services.

At the end of the day the team has a set of technology and user interface freeform sketches that overview an architectural strategy that they believe will work. The diagrams are captured with a smartphone and stored in the project wiki in the architecture handbook section.

## Week Two of Inception

**Patricia meets with the business stakeholders to prioritize the work.** Patricia reviews the story map with the other business stakeholders. They have decided to use DAD's work item list strategy as a backlog of work that will include the stories related to functionality and other work required to produce the solution. They prioritize the cards into a stack representing the work according to the highest business value. Patricia explains to the team that these priorities may need to change somewhat based on the advice of Ashok the architecture owner.

**Terry, Patricia, and Ashok meet to identify an initial list of risks.** Terry and Ashok question Patricia about the non-functional requirements for this solution. How many people will be using this

36

application, during what hours and what are the peak activity periods? How many transactions per hour does she expect? She continues and asks many other questions about reliability, security, performance, and scalability. These non-functional requirements are captured in a list on the whiteboard, but eventually transcribed onto a wiki page that is available to the entire team to reference and update as needed.

Based on the newly identified non-functional requirements, the team evolves their architectural vision and discusses what aspects of the architecture could be the "trickiest" to implement. They capture the key technical risks of the project and brainstorm ways in which they can mitigate these risks. Ideally, mitigating the risk by implementing a piece of functionality related to the risk is preferred but sometimes a technical proof of concept (PoC) known as a "spike" might be used.

**Ashok and Patricia meet to review the prioritized work item list.** With his risk list in hand, Ashok meets with Patricia to review the work priorities. He identifies some parts of the solution that he suggests be moved up to a higher priority in order to mitigate the key technical risks. The strategy is to build an end-to-end working skeleton of the solution that implements these risky, yet still important, requirements early so as to prove the architecture with working code. This will help to remove a lot of the technical risk from the effort early on during Construction, thereby increasing the team's chance of success. Surprisingly, DAD's common-sense approach to mitigation of risk early is not an explicit part of Scrum, often resulting in unpleasant surprises late in projects.

**Patricia and the development team conduct sizing of the work item list.** After considering the strategies in the *Develop Initial Release Plan* goal diagram, the team elects to do estimating with the Planning Poker technique. Since they do not have a deck of planning poker estimation cards they decide to use a planning poker app on their smartphones. The team is already familiar with how to do estimation this way from their DAD workshop last week. They methodically work their way through the stories with the Product Owner describing each story and its acceptance criteria, and subsequently the development team provides an estimate for each. Since this is the first real-world application of this technique for the team, it initially takes some time.

After three hours they are 20% through sizing the stories. Although they have sped up with experience, it's clear that planning poker will take two days in total at their current pace. Carlos suggests a technique called relative mass sizing. Because the team has gotten to the point where they have a common understanding of how to size things, this strategy is now an option for them. They clear off their boardroom table and using masking tape (painter's tape) they section it off into six "size sections", in this case 1, 2, 3, 5, 8, and ?. The question mark section is for stories that are either larger than eight (and will resize later via planning poker), or something that the team needs to discuss further, or something that needs to be reorganized into smaller stories. Each person grabs a subset of the story cards and begins placing them in the size section that they feel is most appropriate. As they're doing this they are also watching how others are placing cards. When they see something that they don't agree with, for example someone else has indicated that a story should be a size three but they think that it's a five, then they say something along the lines of "who thinks this is a three?" and the two people talk it through. The stories are sized by the team in parallel, speeding things up. The team spends an hour and a half sizing the stories, ending up with five that they felt needed to be explored in greater detail. Patricia agrees to work with the stakeholders to flesh out those stories further over the next few days.

**The team creates a release plan.** The team decides that they will go with two-week iterations for the Construction phase. The total relative points for all the work that they estimated summed to 160 points. The team is uncertain as to how many iterations they should plan for the release in order to complete this work. Carlos explains an approach that he has seen work well on other projects. On an agile project we certainly do not want to invest weeks doing detailed estimates on all of the work, but without some idea of what can be completed in an iteration it is difficult to plan. So he suggests that the team invest a half-day planning the work for the first iteration of Construction. After decomposing a set of work items/stories that are planned for the first iteration by creating detailed tasks and estimates for the work, and then doing a sanity check to ensure that the team has enough hours/capacity to complete the work in two weeks, the team can gauge approximately how many points can be delivered in an iteration. Carlos warns

Patricia that it is only an guess since it is difficult to estimate without some actual experience based on this project's team, technology, and other situational-dependent factors. The team decides to spend the next morning estimating.

**Estimating the number of iterations required.** Based on the detailed planning session, the next morning the team determines that they can complete the five-highest priority items from the work item list. These items represent estimates of twenty total relative points. Based on a total of 160 points for the entire backlog, and the expected team's "velocity" of twenty points per iteration, simple division would indicate that it will take eight iterations to complete the application. Carlos suggests that considering the degree of uncertainty on this project related to a new team, technology, and process that some contingency be added to the release plan. He suggests that two iterations be added to the 8 iteration schedule to make the total ten iterations. This allows for unexpected "surprises" including possible additional scope additions that should not jeopardize the ship date of the application. So they agree that the Construction phase will be ten iterations of two weeks. This identifies a date that the business stakeholders can depend on. The greatest frustration that Berhard and other business stakeholders have with IT is their inability to deliver on time. One of the reasons that a disciplined agile approach has been adopted is to address this problem.

As you can see in the goal diagram for *Develop the Initial Release Plan*, an alternative approach would be to set the expectation the system would be released as soon as sufficient functionality is available. This is called a scope-driven approach versus the date-driven approach selected by the team.

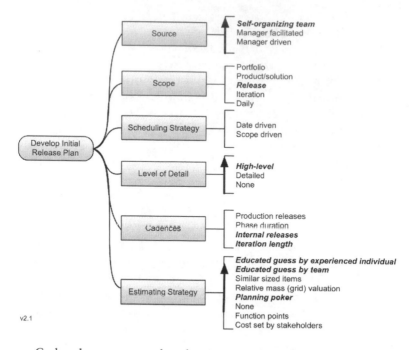

Carlos then suggests that the team agree on the time required to transition to the stakeholders. DAD recognizes that stakeholders include more than just the end users of the application. It also includes groups such as support and maintenance that will be responsible for supporting the solution in production. Carlos advises that the Transition phase be extended beyond the go-live date to allow for a reasonable hand-off period to the support group. They agree that a three-week Transition phase should be sufficient. The release plan also shows three weeks of time for "usage" of the application that BigBank typically calls a warranty period after which they expect the project to be completed. DAD has a milestone called *Delighted Stakeholders* to signify completing the release/project.

Terry creates a high-level Gantt chart to show the release schedule and associated milestones. This schedule will be updated periodically through Construction based on actuals.

INITIAL RELEASE PLAN - MORTGAGE APPLICATION PORTAL (MAP)

| INCEPTION | CONSTRUCTION | | | | | | | | | | TRANSITION | WARRANTY |
|---|---|---|---|---|---|---|---|---|---|---|---|---|
| | C1 | C2 | C3 | C4 | C5 | C6 | C7 | C8 | C9 | C10 | | |

SEPT 4    OCT 2    OCT 30    NOV 27    DEC 25    JAN 22    MAR 4
SEPT 18    OCT 16    NOV 13    DEC 11    JAN 8    FEB 12

Stakeholder Vision

Proven Architecture

Sufficient Functionality

Production Ready

Delighted Stakeholders

## Week Three of Inception

**Terry works with the Facilities group to set up a common work area for the team.** During the last two weeks Terry and Carlos have been scouting the building for a good work area in which to collocate the team. They secure a 24 x 24 foot area which they have christened the "agile pod". During this week they worked with the development team and Patricia to organize desks in a manner that fosters team collaboration. Carlos suggests several layouts based on what he has seen work

in other organizations. The figure here shows what the new work area looks like. The outer walls are high cubicle walls, roughly two meters (6'6") in height, with the exception of the walls at the top, which are one meter in height. In the top-right corner of the pod area there are two large whiteboards as well as space for a manual task board. They will use colored sticky notes to show the progress of their tasks against the iteration's work items. It is in this area that the team will hold their daily stand-up coordination meetings. There is also a whiteboard next to it for ad-hoc modeling. The two little angled rectangles represent whiteboards on wheels. In the top left area the team has a table for team collaborations such as iteration planning, reviews, and retrospectives. A monitor hangs on this wall so that ad-hoc demonstrations to interested stakeholders can take place at any time. It is also useful for other team reviews such as backlog reviews and estimating. The team thinks that they may wish to migrate their manual task board to a virtual board at some point in which case the board will be displayed on this monitor. A key philosophy of creating this pod is to give the team an environment in which they will not need to leave the work area for meetings except in rare situations such as town hall meetings. This fosters team collaboration and focus where team members are expected to be available to help each other at all times.

**Ashok works with the developers to set up the tooling environment.** Beginning late in the first week, the development team starts setting up the development environment and supporting tools. For this project they will use a set of Java-based technologies. In the spirit of allowing the team to self-organize Terry allows each developer to use the IDE of their choice. They install GIT as their source code repository and as a group they develop a source code management and branching strategy. They also set up a build server to automatically create builds upon checking in code changes and to run automated developer regression tests (unit tests). While they would also like to create some scripting to allow testers to self-deploy to a separate testing environment, they run out of time in this phase. They resolve to do this in the first iteration of the Construction phase. They convince Patricia to add the requirement to create deployment scripting to the work item list as a high order work item.

**Terry leads the team to update the risk list.** The team spends about thirty minutes brainstorming potential risks that they face. They capture these risks on the whiteboard initially, rating them on likeliness to occur (percentage) and the likely impact (scale of one to ten) if they do occur. Simple math, the likeliness of occurrence times the likely impact, gives a severity rating that is used to prioritize the risks. After the meeting Terry captures the risk in a spreadsheet which he then prints and puts on the wall beside their task board. The risk list, sorted in priority order, looks like this:

| Risks & Mitigation Strategies | Chance | Impact | Severity |
|---|---|---|---|
| Delivery date for customer web services slips<br>• Ashok to work closely with Team X-Ray to monitor their status | 60% | 8 | 4.8 |
| Stakeholders aren't available<br>• Patricia to work closely with them to ensure availability<br>• Berhard to support Patricia | 30% | 8 | 2.4 |
| Architecture strategy doesn't work<br>• Will prove it in Iteration C1 with working code | 10% | 10 | 1 |
| New versions of our supported browsers will be released<br>• Debbie will monitor release announcements<br>• Team will develop automated test suite | 100% | 1 | 1 |

**Summarizing the Inception work into a vision.** Patricia, Ashok, and Terry work together to consolidate their work for the last three weeks into a vision statement that they can review with stakeholders. They choose to present this work in a PowerPoint presentation. Carlos provides a template from his work on similar teams at other organizations. They create one or two slides to present each of the following topics:

- Business goals of the initiative
- Success Criteria
- Key Stakeholders and Roles
- Vision
  - o Initial Scope of the Project
  - o Initial Technical Strategy
  - o Initial Release Plan
  - o Work Environment details
  - o Initial Project Risks

**The *Stakeholder Vision* milestone review.** At the end of the Inception phase, a review of the vision is conducted with key stakeholders as part of reaching the Stakeholder Vision milestone. The meeting is scheduled for one hour. The entire development team, as well as stakeholders from the business, operations, and support attend the meeting. Additionally, other interested stakeholders attend from enterprise architecture, technical documentation, training, internal audit, and project management office (PMO). Although such a large group might not attend each Inception milestone review, they should at least be given the opportunity to review the vision so that there are no nasty surprises later in the project.

Patricia, Terry, and Ashok present parts of their Inception findings. Twenty minutes are reserved for questions from the stakeholders.

Terry and Patricia conclude the meeting by asking for "general agreement," sufficient to achieve the Stakeholder Vision goal and thus proceed into the Construction phase on Monday.

Berhard the business sponsor and Victoria the VP of IT commend the team on their excellent work in Inception and agree that the project as framed seems reasonable. Carlos reminds everyone that while the Vision gets the stakeholders and team on the same page and gets everyone going in a common direction, the vision will be revisited at the end of each iteration to ensure that the project is unfolding as described in this meeting. The meeting adjourns. The team is excited about starting Construction on Monday. They agree that investing three weeks doing high-level planning and modeling was a good use of time.

The team spends the remainder of the day moving from their current desks into their new desks in the agile pod. They are genuinely excited about coming back into work on Monday morning.

# 6 CONSTRUCTION ITERATION C1

After a short, lightweight Inception phase where the team invested the time to gain agreement around the approach that they are going to take, they are ready to begin Construction. Note that it is impossible to devote as much space in this book as needed to comprehensively cover what happened in this team. Therefore we describe key events and issues that were encountered and the strategies that the team took to address them. The transparency built into the agile process combined with constant self-evaluation by the team quickly surfaces problems so that they can be fixed in a timely and open manner. Also keep in mind that this project has chosen to use the Agile/Basic (Scrum-based) DAD lifecycle. For a different lifecycle the experiences would be quite different.

**Day 1.** Normally the team would spend the first half of day one of the iteration conducting an iteration planning session. However, since the team invested some time in Inception to plan the first iteration in order to improve the quality of their estimates for the purposes of release planning, the planning for this iteration is already done.

There are six stories, which total twenty points. Three of the stories address technically significant functionality that when implemented will prove that the team's architectural strategy (identified during Inception) will actually work. There is a chance that the team will discover that the strategy doesn't work and in that

| Customer can view the portal landing page in browser | Customer can request online credit check * |
| Customer can create draft mortgage application * | Customer can view MAP landing page on mobile phone |
| Mortgage specialist can approve basic mortgage application * | Customer can get list of existing mortgages |

\* Technically Risky

case they will need to evolve their architectural approach based on their learning. This is an aspect of DAD's risk-value lifecycle strategy where technical risk is considered when prioritizing the work, leading to the Proven Architecture milestone early in Construction.

They do however need to create their task board. On the white board in the corner of their new pod they create columns for Not Started, In Progress, Needs Validation, and Completed. Carlos points out that in his experience different teams customize the names and types of columns based on what they think is most effective but these columns are good ones with which to start. The team then creates sticky notes representing each work item/story and puts them in the left column going down in priority order.

| STORY/ WORK ITEMS | NOT STARTED | IN PROGRESS | NEEDS VALIDATION | COMPLETE | HOURS REMAINING |
|---|---|---|---|---|---|
| Customer can view the portal landing page in browser | | | | | 45 |
| Customer can request online credit check | | | | | 45 |
| Customer can create draft mortgage application | | | | | 60 |
| Customer can view MAP landing page on mobile phone | | | | | 30 |
| Mortgage specialist can approve basic mortgage application | | | | | 40 |
| Customer can get list of existing mortgages | | | | | 20 |
| | | | | TOTAL HOURS REMAINING | 240 |

They then have a coordination meeting to plan the day's work. Each team member takes one or two stickies for the tasks that they intend to work on today and move them to the "In Progress" column. They ensure that these tasks have their initials on them so that it is clear who is working on each task. Adding up the total hours on all the sticky notes the team comes up with at total of 240 hours of work to be completed over the ten-day iteration. The team understands that unexpected work will arise during the iteration so they have ensured that the 240 hours is about 20% less than their total available hours to allow for contingency.

Terry facilitates the meeting, asking each team member to describe what they plan to do today, if anything is slowing them down or blocking their progress, and if they need help from anyone to complete their work.

After the coordination meeting, Terry creates an Iteration burndown chart on a piece of flip chart paper and pins it next to the team's task board to help keep the team on track to complete all the work that they have committed to for this iteration. The burndown shows 240 hours of work remaining and will be updated everyday as hours are reduced by work being completed.

During the day Terry books an Iteration Review meeting with the stakeholders to be held the following Friday afternoon at the end of the iteration. He also books a meeting with the team to follow this review known as a retrospective to discuss the iteration results and how the team can improve.

**Day 2.** The team gathers around the task board for their daily coordination meeting at 9:00 sharp. Terry reminds the team that although yesterday's meeting ran for about thirty minutes, the goal moving forward is to keep the meeting to under fifteen minutes. Terry also points out a new sheet that he has pinned next to the task board that describes his proposal for a Definition of Done (DoD). He explains that for each of the work items on the board it is important that everyone understand what being "done" really means. The sheet looks like this:

Definition of Done (DoD)
- All code tested and checked in
- All unit tests passing
- All acceptance tests written and accepted as passed
- Usability standards met
- Peer reviews completed
- Architecture handbook updated if necessary

This sheet will serve as a reminder that there is more to considering a work item being done than the code running and some basic testing being complete. The team discusses the proposed DoD and the implications for how they're going to work. During the discussion Danny points out that Terry had forgotten to include the need to update the help screens to reflect changes to the solution. The DoD is updated accordingly, and it's expected that the DoD will evolve as the team learns more about the needs of their stakeholders.

As each team member gives their update for what they

accomplished yesterday, what they plan to do today, and if they have any "blockers" to their work Terry tracks how many hours the team has reduced on the task board. Once Ashok, Debbie, and Danny have given their updates, Terry provides his own update. Adding up the hours that the four of them have reduced off the tasks he comes up with fifteen hours in total. However, as the burndown chart shows, in order for the team to reduce the total of 240 hours to zero by the end of the iteration the team needs to burndown twenty-four hours per day. Terry brings this to the attention of the team and says, "We didn't get as much done yesterday as we had hoped but I understand since we are all new to this process. Additionally I know that we were spending some time on activities not on our task board such as tuning our build scripts and other setup related to our development environments. So as the iteration plan shows, we have fallen nine hours behind. As a team we'll need to figure out how to get back on track."

**Day 3.** During the daily coordination meeting some issues surface. Danny says that he is struggling with his current task that he originally estimated would take three hours. He can't seem to figure out how to solve a technical issue and he also thinks that his estimate was far too low. Not only did he make no progress but he thinks that there are six hours still remaining. Terry explains that this is not unusual and luckily the team has some contingency in the iteration plan for unplanned work. Terry asks someone to volunteer to pair with Ashok to get over this technical hurdle. Unfortunately no one volunteers because they are most concerned about falling behind on their own work. Carlos the Coach steps in and reminds the team that getting all the work done in order to meet their commitments to the Product Owner is everyone's responsibility. Debbie speaks up and volunteers to help Danny. As a result of increasing the estimate

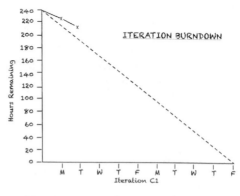

for Danny's task and not making progress, the team actually only burned down ten hours instead of the expected twenty-four. The burndown shows that the team is quickly falling behind.

While this is a definitely a problem the good news is that using a chart like this exposes scheduling problems immediately and makes it transparent to the whole team. Danny volunteers to stay late tonight to try to get back on track. The rest of the team decides to stay and help out. Ashok can't stay as he needs to pick up his son from daycare but promises to dial in on the VPN later this evening to work on his tasks.

**Days 4-7.** The team continues work and makes up for most of the time lost. However it looks like they will not get all six stories completed by the end of the iteration.

**Day 8.** During the daily coordination meeting the on eighth day the team discusses what to do about the fact that they will not meet their commitment of the planned work for this iteration. Carlos advises that it is better to get as many work items "done" according to the definition of done that is posted rather than 80% done on each story but nothing completely done. The team decides to stop work on *Basic application approval*, which Danny had just started working on yesterday afternoon, and focus on completing the other five work items. They notify Patricia, the Product Owner, immediately so that she can inform the stakeholders and thus retain team transparency.

Dick, the DBA, is skeptical about working in an agile manner even after the DAD training the team received. Throughout the iteration he has paired with people whenever any database development was needed, such as creating a new table or adding columns to an existing table, but each time he does so he has complained about wanting to do the entire database design up front. During the coordination meeting today he identified this as a blocker, and Carlos offers to discuss agile strategies for database development with him after the meeting. This conversation doesn't go well, even though Carlos shared stories about previous experiences on other teams in similar circumstances. Dick decides that he knows best, and decides to secretly work on detailed logical and physical data models in his spare time so as to "save the team" when it discovers that he is right after all.

**Day 9.** Ashok and Debbie pair together to implement the *Save draft application* story, one of the three key stories that help to prove that the team's architecture strategy is sound. Early that week

Ashok completed work on *Request online credit check*, also a technically critical story. The previous day the team chose to drop *Basic application approval* from the current iteration, the third technically critical story. As a result the team will be unable to fully prove that their architecture works until at least Iteration C2. Terry works with Patricia to cancel the existing milestone review meeting (scheduled for tomorrow) and tentatively reschedule it into the same time slot at the end of Iteration C2. They also send out an email explaining why the review needs to be rescheduled.

**Day 10.** The team spends the morning stabilizing the work items/stories that they have completed, doing exploratory testing, and fixing last minute defects.

**The iteration review.** In the afternoon an iteration review is held with the stakeholders. The DAD framework suggests that this review should be more than just a demonstration. It also makes sense to review the project status against the vision that was agreed to at the end of the Inception phase. As such, Terry has prepared a simple presentation to cover the following topics:

- Set the context: Where are we in relationship to the release plan?
- Iteration results: Did the team deliver all the work items that they committed to?
- Team performance: What is the throughput of the team (velocity)? Is quality good?
- Solution demonstration
- Update on the vision:
  - Are we on track? Based on the velocity trend of the team, can we deliver according to the dates from the Inception release plan?
  - What is the status of the outstanding risks?
  - When will the architecture be proven?
  - Are there any issues that need to be addressed?
  - Q & A

The team isn't entirely confident that the new functionality would work as expected during the demo since the application was periodically crashing during testing. So Ashok insists on doing the demo so that Patricia won't break it. Carlos lets the team conduct the demo this way but says that he wants to discuss the approach during the retrospective after the iteration review meeting. Sure enough, the demo crashes when the last new feature is being demonstrated. The stakeholders poke fun at the team and they feel a bit embarrassed. Nevertheless the stakeholders are still impressed that they saw some working software only two weeks into the project. They did say that they are a bit disappointed that the team didn't meet its commitment on all the functionality. Carlos mentions that this is a common pattern for new agile teams in that they tend to be overly optimistic during their estimating. Agile is new to the team and it will take a few iterations for them to learn to work effectively together and be certain that they are making commitments that they can keep.

**The retrospective.** After the meeting ends the team stays behind to have their retrospective meeting. Carlos facilitates the meeting, asking each team member to describe what they thought went well, what didn't go well, and some ideas for how the team can improve its performance. The discusses the following issues:

- Terry feels that the team did a great job for a team new to agile doing their first iteration. Carlos agrees.

- Tara expresses concern that the burden of the testing was on her shoulders and most of the stories were not available for proper testing until the seventh day of the iteration. She didn't have time to cover as many test cases as she had hoped. The team agrees to pitch in and help with the testing more, and to test one anothers' work, not just their own. They also decided that they need to try to build the stories in priority order and make them available to Tara and Patricia as early as possible in the iteration.

- Danny admits that he should have asked for help with his technical issues earlier. The team agrees that they should try more pairing when developing tricky parts of the solution.

- The team recognizes that they are still new to continuous integration (CI) and that they need to work on their approach a bit more.

- The team was only able to deliver sixteen instead of the twenty points of work that they had intended. They decided that they should only commit to sixteen points for the next iteration, and take on additional work if they finish this work with time to spare. Fortunately, with two contingency iterations, the team can still deliver all functionality according to the planned dates in the Release Plan.

- The team recognizes that they should have fleshed out the high-priority items on the backlog a bit better so as to have a smoother planning session. The team realizes that they will suffer from the same problem the next day when they plan the next iteration. Patricia commits to doing some look-ahead analysis modeling each iteration from now on, and Ashok similarly commits to leading team members in doing look-ahead design modeling. Carlos points out that this is sometimes called backlog grooming or backlog refinement in Scrum, although DAD prefers clearer terminology such as look-ahead modeling.

As a result of the retrospective the team develops a hand-written list of improvements which they captured on their whiteboard. Realizing that they likely can't implement all of the improvements immediately, they decided to prioritize them so that they can focus on implementing a few key improvements at a time. Displaying their list publicly as an information radiator helps to keep the improvement plan in everyone's mind.

# 7 CONSTRUCTION ITERATION C2

**Iteration planning session.** The team comes in Monday morning refreshed and ready to start a new iteration. Patricia walks the team through the highest priority work items that collectively add up to 16 points. For each story, she explains the functionality and the acceptance criteria. She has brought a few screen mockups to the planning session that she shares with the team. The mockups are a good start, but as they found during the first iteration they aren't sufficient. For two of the stories she finds that she needs to draw a flow chart to describe the business logic supporting the story. She also takes time to describe several business terms, often to respond to questions from Dick who likes to understand these sorts of things. The other team members also find that these conversations have helped to clarify several concepts about which they were unsure.

For each story, Ashok leads the team in a discussion regarding the technical strategy that they will take to implement it. Based on this "just in time" design, the team identifies its development and testing tasks in a similar way to the last iteration. At several points Danny and Ashok work through an idea on the whiteboard while others provide input. Although this modeling proves to be of value, the team realizes that it adds time to their planning session.

Since the team is now more familiar with the process, the planning session goes a bit smoother than it did in the previous iteration. However, it takes longer than expected due to the need to work through the business logic and implementation details. This further reinforces their decision to start doing look-ahead modeling each iteration, one of the learnings identified in their retrospective last iteration. Terry volunteers to clean up the task board from the previous iteration and set up the board with the new work items and tasks. After lunch the team is ready to jump in and start working on the items

**Days 1 to 5.** The team starts doing the work required to implement the stories, including the story they didn't complete in Iteration C1, that they've picked for this two-week iteration. Although everyone is sitting together in the agile pod, they are still working (for the most part) separately. Whenever someone runs into a difficultly, such as how to specifically write a section of code, they ask someone else for help. Danny, Debbie, and Terry typically ask Ashok for help as he has many years of development experience. Every so often a team member asks Patricia or Barbara to do a bit of just in time (JIT) modeling with them to work through the details of some business logic or how a user interface feature should behave.

Dick continues to pair with other team members on database functionality when needed. He also continues to work on the detailed data model and pretty much finishes it this week.

Tara and Carlos work on getting the team's continuous integration (CI) strategy up and running. Carlos has done this sort of thing before and Tara is eager to learn more as she is intrigued about how automated regression testing fits in. Furthermore Tara has little testing work to do this week while she waits for other team members to sufficiently complete their work before she can start hers. Although the others on the team are doing their best to write unit tests, it certainly isn't their strong point. Tara feels that this isn't how the team should be approaching testing so she brings it up with Carlos. Carlos agrees and tells her that this is an issue he intended to bring up with the team once the CI infrastructure is in place. He also suggests that improvement suggestions might be better coming from her, and that she should think about it a bit.

The daily coordination meetings each morning are starting to run better, although often last twenty or even twenty-five minutes instead of the desired ten to fifteen. Some people, particularly Danny, tend to show up late for the meeting, forcing people to wait. Both Ashok and Debbie, and sometimes Terry, go into too much detail and often try to start solving problems during the meeting instead of waiting until afterwards. Danny suffers from the opposite problem in that his updates are often too short and miss important information that other team members need to know. Carlos gently coaches the team every day on these issues.

On the fifth day Carlos takes Danny aside and asks him why he's often late. Danny says he has trouble getting up some mornings and besides that he doesn't think that there's much value in the coordination meetings anyway. Carlos describes to him why it's important that everyone attend on-time and be prepared. He asks Danny to do so just like all the rest of the team members. Danny agrees but Carlos can tell that Danny still isn't fully convinced.

**Day 6.** Patricia and Barbara the business analyst spend two hours in the afternoon doing some look-ahead modeling with several stakeholders, including Berhard, to explore the next eight highest-priority stories on the work item list. In the process of doing this they create a collection of hand-drawn screen sketches, a flow chart overviewing the business process supported by the stories, and several business rules definitions which they capture as point-form text. After the modeling session Patricia decides to schedule a recurring meeting in this time slot to perform look-ahead analysis. Her intention is to invite the appropriate stakeholders two weeks in advance as she realizes that the people she needs to work with will vary each time.

**Day 7.** Debbie, with the help of Ashok, finishes work on the *Basic application approval* story that had been dropped from the previous iteration. With this work accomplished the team has done sufficient work to prove that their architecture strategy works via working code. After a quick review by Terry to verify that they have met the acceptance criteria for *Basic application approval,* he is confident that he can safely confirm the light-weight milestone review meeting that had been tentatively scheduled for Day 10.

**Day 10.** As with the first iteration, the team spends most of the morning on hardening activities. Patricia prepares for the demo, practicing several scenarios with the working solution that will show the new functionality that was implemented this iteration. Ashok and Terry meet for half an hour to finalize their strategy for the milestone review meeting in the afternoon.

**The demo**. The demo goes much better this iteration for two reasons: First, the team completed all of the work that they had committed to at the beginning of the iteration, which pleased Berhard. In this iteration the team delivered a total of nineteen points which is an improvement over the sixteen delivered in iteration C1. Carlos explained that it is common to see a team's velocity increase during the first few iterations as the team becomes more efficient and implements its own process improvements from their retrospectives. Second, Patricia was much more comfortable running the demo this time. Patricia invited to the demo two business stakeholders, Kristen and Rod, who had been involved with initial requirements modeling but who hadn't yet seen what the team had produced to date. During the demo they are excited about what they see but are perplexed as to why there is so little to see. Although Patricia and Berhard have explained the new agile approach to them, they didn't realize at first that they would only see a partially complete solution. Once they get over this misunderstanding they begin to suggest new ideas for what could be built. Patricia tells them about the next modeling session in a week and a half and invites them to be involved. Kristen and Rod promise to make room in their schedules and more importantly to think some more about what they really want the solution to do.

**The *Proven Architecture* milestone review**. Ashok walks Enrico the enterprise architect, Oliver the Operations Manager, and Chris the CSM through the working solution. The rest of the team, including Patricia, also attend this review to be available to answer any questions that may arise and hopefully to pick up some insights into how architects think. Ashok's focus is on working through three stories: *Save draft application*; *Request online credit check*; and *Basic application approval*. These stories represent an end-to-end working skeleton of the solution that proves the architecture works. Ashok explains these stories to the stakeholders, walking through how the implementation of the stories stresses the architecture in a meaningful way. He does this by sketching the architecture solution on the whiteboard as he describes each story. Enrico asks a few pointed questions regarding how Ashok's strategy fits into the company's overall technology roadmap.

Ashok replies that it's the team's architectural strategy, not just his, and then goes on to describe how during Inception the team's architecture modeling was influenced by the roadmap. Patricia points out that the scoping effort was similarly influenced by the business roadmap.

Towards the end of the review Chris questions why the *Request online credit check* story was implemented this early in the project. Patricia jumps in, saying that the story was in fact a medium-priority requirement originally, but that Ashok convinced her to move it to the top of the work item list so as to prove the architecture. Chris says that's exactly the issue that he's bringing up, saying that Scrum teams would work in business priority value. Ashok replies that an advantage of Disciplined Agile Delivery is that it focuses on risk reduction early in the lifecycle, including both business and technical risk. Enrico and Oliver both agree that this strategy is much better than what they've seen with Scrum teams in the past, saying that they have a much better understanding of what the team is actually doing and are impressed that they not only thought through important architectural issues but can actually show that they work. Enrico observes that this has worked better than the onerous architecture reviews that many of BigBank's traditional development teams are still doing.

**The retrospective**. Terry leads the retrospective, starting it by asking everyone to discuss what they feel is going well. Overall people are happy with how things are going. They like the more collaborative style of working and everyone has an anecdote about how they learned something from someone else through working closely with them. Everyone is relieved that both the iteration demo and the milestone review went well, although there is a bit of concern about how the requirements may expand given the exuberance of the stakeholders during the demo. The team also reviews their improvement list from the previous iteration and discusses where they've made some headway.

When Terry asks people where they need to improve it becomes clear that quality is the main issue. Carlos points out that the need to spend so much time to harden at the end of the iteration is an indication that the team isn't testing sufficiently, and of course fixing any problems, early in the iteration. Danny says that sometimes he needs to code for a few days before he has anything suitable for Tara to test. Carlos points out that the team is currently following a strategy called "testless programming" where developers write a bunch of code and then ask someone else to test it for them. Debbie claims that her and Danny are doing some unit testing as they code, which Carlos says is a good start but that it's possible for the developers to do more testing themselves and thereby reduce the overall cost and time to fix any problems with their code. Carlos walks the team through the goal diagram for *Produce a Potentially Consumable Solution* which is shown below.

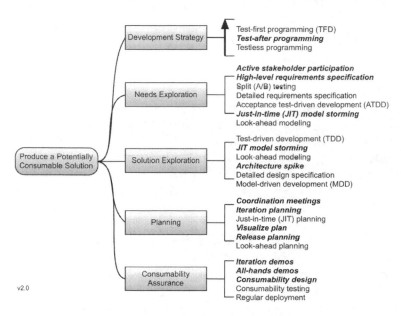

As you can see, the DAD framework supports two other, more effective approaches to programming: Test-after programming where people write a little bit of code and then test it thoroughly (ideally writing automated regression tests when doing so) and test-first (or test-driven) programming where you write a single test and then just enough production code to fulfill that test. After a bit of discussion about the advantages and disadvantages of each approach, the team decides to try a test-after approach going forward. Although a test-first approach would be preferable, the team feels that they don't yet have the discipline to make it work. Carlos points out that once the team gets good at test-after programming, they should then consider taking the next improvement step to a test-first strategy. Tara offers to be available to pair with people while they are writing code to help them to work in a test-after manner. Carlos brings up how the team's continuous integration (CI) strategy is operational but the team isn't taking full advantage of it yet. Everyone agrees and Carlos commits to working with everyone next week to give them some one-on-one coaching in CI.

Danny asks whether the team should take on more points of work in the next iteration since in this iteration they completed nineteen points versus their estimated velocity of sixteen. Carlos recommended tracking their velocity trend for one or two more iterations before changing the expected velocity and adjusting the release plan forecast.

The team finishes the day by updating their "management artifacts". The risk list is updated to show that the architecture has been proven and accepted by the appropriate stakeholders. The team also adds the risk that the requirements may expand given the positive feedback received during the demo.

Mark Lines and Scott W. Ambler

# 8 CONSTRUCTION ITERATION C3

Construction Iteration C3 begins on an uptick. The team is excited because the second iteration was successful and general consensus is that this will be the same for this iteration. Terry leads the team through iteration planning, which takes a bit less than three hours. This is much faster than what has happened in the past, and it's due in part from the team's greater experience with iteration planning but mostly due to the look-ahead modeling efforts lead by Patricia and Ashok.

The daily coordination meetings are running much better. Everyone is showing up on time and for the most part staying focused on coordinating their day instead of trying to solve problems in the meeting. Danny is still struggling, however, to participate effectively in the meetings.

**Day 2**. During the team coordination meeting both Danny and Debbie ask Tara if she has some time to pair with them, separately, to help them test their work. To do this Tara sits right beside a developer and pairs with them to write both production code and the unit tests to validate that new code. After a bit of time to get used to it, Tara and the developer swap the keyboard regularly, talk through the logic of how to test something, and most importantly learn new skills and ways of thinking from each other. Throughout the rest of the iteration Tara spends about two-thirds of her time pairing with either Danny, Debbie, Ashok, or Terry in this manner. The other third of her time is spent on other forms on testing, including functional, integration, and stress testing. During the iteration planning session the day before Tara had indicated to the team that she had intended to spend most of her time pairing with others to help them test.

**Day 6**. Early in the afternoon Patricia leads a look-ahead modeling session with several stakeholders to explore upcoming requirements. During this session the stakeholders not only describe how the stories for the upcoming iteration should work they also identify several new stories and drop a few of the low priority requirements. These changes result in what looks to be a 20% increase in scope.

Patricia goes to Carlos in a bit of a panic, asking for help to deal with this "scope creep." Having worked with IT teams before, albeit ones following a traditional approach, Patricia is worried that this increase in scope will put the team at risk. Carlos points out that a big spike in new requirements early in Construction is quite common on agile teams. It is the natural result of greater stakeholder participation – when you produce a consumable solution on a regular basis, show it to people, and ask for their feedback you typically get it. It's healthy for the requirements to evolve as it increases the chance that the team will build something the stakeholders actually want as opposed to something built to specification.

**Day 7.** During the daily coordination meeting Patricia informs the team about the new requirements. Terry suggests that the team spend some time today to have Patricia walk through the new requirements so that the team can determine the actual impact. The team decides to do this immediately following lunch. Patricia begins the session describing the changes and the reasons behind them. After a bit of discussion around how to implement the new stories the team is convinced that the new requirements will not impact their architecture strategy at all. They decide that this is due to the initial modeling they did during the Inception phase.

Terry leads the team through sizing the new requirements using the relative mass sizing technique, taking about thirty minutes to do so. The total time for the impact assessment meeting was a bit more than one and a half hours. After this everyone on the team, except for Terry and Patricia, goes back to work. Terry and Patricia work together to update the burnup chart, which now shows that the team is likely to need twelve Construction iterations in total. Because Berhard, the project sponsor, has made it clear that the schedule is firm Patricia realizes that she needs to call a meeting to rethink which requirements are "must haves" for this release and which can wait for a future release.

**Day 8**. During the coordination meeting Terry and Danny discover that they both worked on the same functionality the previous morning. Although this was a bit frustrating for both of them, for Danny it was a valuable lesson in why everyone needs to actively participate in team coordination meetings.

**Day 9**. Patricia facilitates a one-hour meeting with Berhard and the stakeholders who were involved with the modeling session on day 6. During the meeting she negotiates with them to allocate some of the lower priority requirements to be implemented in the next release. Fortunately management has learned that treating this initiative as a series of releases similar to a typical product management strategy is a better approach than funding one project. Knowing that there will be more funding allocated to a future release makes these scope negotiations much easier. About 70% of the requirements, including most of the new ones, are marked as "must haves" for the first release. All others are marked as "nice to have" that ideally will be implemented in the first release although if they get pushed to a future release the stakeholders will accept it. This categorization will enable the team to make their delivery date. Terry also attends the meeting to represent the team, but for the most part spends his time listening to the discussion.

**Day 10**. The team finds that it has much less hardening to perform during this iteration. This is due to doing more testing earlier in the lifecycle. The demo goes very well. The stakeholders like what they're seeing and feel very optimistic about the progress being made. This sense of optimism is new to them as their previous experiences working with IT have always been problematic. Due to the degree of their active participation in the project and through regular demonstrations they realize that they are less likely to encounter nasty surprises late in the project which has been typical in the past.

Terry shares the updated burnup chart with the team. The chart now shows two requirement lines, one showing the number of "must have" points and the other showing the grand total of points. Patricia describes to the team what

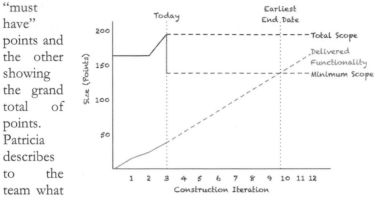

happened during the prioritization session with the stakeholders the day before. Terry then explains that with the new version of the burnup chart that the point where their burnup line meets the must-have line is the earliest time that they can decide to release their work into production. At this point they will be completely done all of the requested work. This is known in DAD as the *Sufficient Functionality* milestone.

**The retrospective**. The team begins with a review of how they're doing with implementing the process improvements from previous iterations. Their approach to testing has clearly improved although they have much more work to do. The iteration planning session went smoother this time and everyone hopes it will be even better next iteration. Team coordination meetings are also going better each day as well, although they sometimes last up to twenty minutes still so there is still room for improvement.

Ashok says that he's a bit worried about the level of documentation that the team is producing. A few days earlier Oliver, the manager of the operations team, asked Ashok whether the team had started to work on the system overview documentation that's required as part of the overall solution. Ashok said that the team had been capturing notes and photos of diagrams in their team wiki but had not yet started developing any form of "deliverable documentation." Although they're still early in Construction, Ashok feels that they really should be evolving the supporting documentation along with the software that they're building. This reflects DAD's philosophy of developing consumable solutions, not just working software. Carlos suggests that the team adopt the practice of continuous documentation where they write the supporting documentation in parallel to writing the code. He suggests that this can be done in the wiki, and that all the team needs to do is invest a bit more effort to capture sufficient information there. Carlos also offers to pair with anyone needing help to do so.

On a related note Dick reveals that he's been maintaining a detailed data model so far. Danny jokes that this was a well-known secret because everyone on the team knew this was going on. Dick admits that he thinks he's wasted a lot of time maintaining this detailed model. The requirement spike earlier in the week caused him to do a couple of hours of rework on his model, some of which was removing data structures that were no longer needed due to dropped functionality. He's come to realize that evolving the database schema via database refactoring techniques is very safe and straightforward, removing the need for up-front detailed data modeling. Instead he's going to perform database design work on a just-in-time (JIT) basis from now on.

Mark Lines and Scott W. Ambler

# 9 CONSTRUCTION ITERATION C7

It is the seventh Construction iteration and the team is working smoothly. During iterations four through six the team successfully evolved the Mortgage Application Portal (MAP) application, adding new value to it every two weeks. They consistently worked together to learn from each other and to improve their approach based on the ideas they generated each retrospective. There were a few bumps along the way, in particular there were a few heated discussions between team members when disagreements arose as to how to implement certain features. Luckily Ashok led the team through these hard technical decisions, exactly as an Architecture Owner should.

**Stakeholder collaboration.** The stakeholders are very happy with the progress that is being made and are regularly giving feedback to the team during both scheduled and impromptu modeling sessions as well as demos. Patricia is comfortable in her position as product owner and is finding the role both rewarding and challenging. It can be hard at times for her to get access to the right stakeholders as they have their "real jobs" to do. And of course the stakeholders all have differing opinions and goals, making it difficult for her at times to negotiate requirement priorities with them. Requirements are still evolving, with new ones being added all the time, which is a natural consequence of regular stakeholder participation.

Patricia and Berhard begin working with Mindy's team to develop a marketing strategy for MAP. This is the first time that Mindy's team has had to develop a strategy for a customer-facing solution that will be regularly released in small increments. Mindy is very excited about working in an agile manner because it feels natural to her. Mindy asks Patricia to arrange some training for her staff to ensure that they understand how agile works and what they need to do to interact effectively with the development team. Patricia asks Terry and Carlos to run a two-hour training session for Mindy's marketing team, and both Patricia and Mindy attend the training to help underscore the importance to BigBank of this new approach. Mindy's team will work closely with Patricia and Terry from now on to ensure that the marketing strategy is synchronized with what the development team is doing. The plan is to begin the marketing campaign a few days after the system is released into production.

**Test often, test early**. Danny, Debbie, and Terry have all increased their testing skills through pairing with Tara. Lately Tara has been working with Barbara, the business analyst, to automate acceptance tests. Progress was slow at first because Barbara has always captured detailed requirements in documents, but she is now starting to see the value in capturing these details in the form of executable tests. Tara also works with Dick to create and maintain test data.

On the technical side of things the team's continuous integration (CI) strategy is working very well for them. During Iteration C5 the team's test suite was too slow due to the growing number of regression tests. The team's solution was to create a test suite that would run in five minutes or less on their work stations. This test suite focused on functionality developed the previous iteration as well as new functionality this iteration. To help speed up the tests that run on people's workstations, Dick introduced database mocks during Iteration C6. A second test suite is run in their team integration sandbox which takes about thirty minutes in total. This test suite runs every time someone promotes new code into that environment. There is a third test suite that runs once a night. This test suite takes several hours and it includes stress tests and end-to-end integration tests.

**Automated deployment scripts**. The team has developed a script to automatically deploy their working build into a demo environment. This script runs when the nightly build is successful. The script removes the system from the demo environment, including the database, and then rebuilds everything from scratch in the demo environment. The team is thinking of reworking this script for use in deploying into production.

As far as the database goes, Dick evolves the database schema as needed and lately has been actively pairing with others so that they can learn fundamental database skills from him. His comprehensive data model is still being updated by him, but he decides to give up on all the up-front modeling and removes details that are not yet implemented.

**Automated dashboard**. During Iteration C4 the team began to take advantage of the dashboard functionality provided by their development tools. As they do their work the development tools are recording key events, such as whether a build was successful, when the build ran, how many tests ran, and so on. This web-based team dashboard shows graphs generated from this event data. The team started using the dashboard in their own browsers and at the suggestion of Carlos the DAD coach, Terry set up the dashboard to display on the team's monitor on the wall. This strategy is something that DAD refers to as development intelligence, an application of business intelligence (BI) technologies for software delivery teams.

**Planning**. The team has firmly committed to a delivery date based on ten Construction iterations. The previous iteration it looked as if they would reach the point of having delivered sufficient functionality by the end of Iteration C9 but Patricia and Terry agreed that they would rather have that tenth iteration as buffer space. If worse came to worst they would simply implement a bit more functionality than the bare minimum that was required.

The team is also getting serious about deployment planning. They are working very closely with Oliver the operations manager and Samira the support manager to ensure that their teams are ready to accept the new Mortgage Application Portal (MAP) being developed by the team. They have negotiated the release window that they are aiming for with Oliver – At BigBank you can only deploy into Production on Saturday or Sunday between 3am and 5am. They have also started planning how they are going to train Samira's help desk people. Samira's group has a training team that focuses on exactly this type of work. Terry offers to work with this training team to ensure that the training materials will be developed in time.

The team has kept the deliverable documentation up-to-date since Iteration C4 via a continuous documentation strategy. This documentation includes a system overview, online help pages for end-users, an online support guide, and technical release notes.

**The retrospective**. Terry tells the team that Padma, the lead of the Project Management Office (PMO) which Terry still needs to report into, has asked him to stop updating the Gantt chart. She says that the information she is interested in is captured well on the burnup chart but not on the Gantt chart. This is a pleasant surprise for Terry as he didn't expect that Padma would be receptive to agile reporting strategies.

Due to the improvements made in the way that the team

approaches quality there has been very little hardening effort at the end of the last two iterations. Debbie asks if there's a way that the team can use this newly available time effectively. Carlos brings up the idea of doing iteration planning for the next iteration on the last day of the previous one, effectively putting all the management overhead activities on one day. This is something the team decides to try for the rest of the Construction iterations.

# 10 CONSTRUCTION ITERATION C10

This is the last Construction iteration before Transition. Everything is running smoothly within the team.

The focus of this iteration is to implement the high-priority stories that were identified the previous iteration and on hardening the solution. During Iteration C9 Tara shifted her focus from helping the team with unit testing and automated acceptance testing to testing in BigBank's pre-production environment. Tara wanted access to this environment much earlier but BigBank has limited resources for this sort of testing. By working with the pre-production test team she found several system integration challenges that her team wasn't able to simulate up until now. Tara also invests time to thoroughly test the deployment scripts within the pre-production testing environment.

The team chooses to capture these defects as new work items which are prioritized and put on the work item list. Each defect is assigned a size of zero so that they are not counted towards the team's velocity. The decision was based on the recognition that from the point of view of the stakeholders the team should have found and addressed these problems before claiming that the original work was "done". The team finds this a bit frustrating but realize that this is a learning experience for them. Carlos points out that having to spend an iteration or more hardening a solution is a common anti-pattern for teams new to agile.

Terry asks Tara to track the defects, by severity, in a simple spreadsheet. She tracks the severity of the issue, the date it was identified, a brief description, and the date it was resolved. This information is then summarized in a defect trend chart. Tara has done this sort of thing before using more sophisticated defect tracking tools, but finds that the spreadsheet approach is sufficient for their needs right now. The defect trend chart is reviewed as part of the team coordination meeting each morning.

**Day 3**. During the morning Terry reviews the deployment plan with Oliver and Samira. This plan describes how the team will work with Oliver's operations team to deploy the solution into production. The plan also indicates how the support team, managed by Samira, will be trained in time for the deployment. This training needs to occur over several days because only a few help desk staff can be trained at any given time (the rest need to continue providing support to BigBank customers and staff members).

That afternoon Terry and Patricia meet with Mindy, the VP of Marketing, and Mary-Jane, who works for Mindy, to finalize the overall release schedule with her. The four have been meeting for thirty minutes on a weekly basis to coordinate the activities between the two teams. Mary-Jane has been attending the iteration demos and has been actively working with Patricia to ensure that the marketing message reflects what the team is building.

**Day 6**. Patricia cancels her regular look-ahead modeling session and instead spends the time crafting an email with Terry to communicate the release date to the stakeholder community. Although key stakeholders have known about the target release date for a while the wider stakeholder community only knew that it was coming soon. This email indicates the intended release date, a description of what MAP does, an overview of why this is important to BigBank, and an indication of when to expect further communications. This email is submitted to Berhard (the business sponsor) and Victoria (the VP of IT) for their review. The following day they jointly send it out to their constituents.

**Day 10**. Patricia decides to run a two-hour demonstration of the overall solution to the stakeholders. Where previous demos have focused on the new functionality implemented that iteration, this demo walks people through critical, end-to-end functionality of the entire solution. Patricia invited everyone who had attended a demo in the past and most are able to attend. The goal of this demo is to both communicate what the team has accomplished and to verify that they have in fact produced sufficient functionality to justify releasing the solution into production. During the demo several of the stakeholders indicate that they would like more functionality than what is currently implemented, and Patricia asks them whether they can wait until a future release for that functionality. Two of the stakeholders are unhappy with that idea because they have heard this promise before from IT only to find out that the next release is years away. Berhard states that the plan is to get just enough functionality into production now so as to get to market quickly and that they fully intend to start into the next release once this one is successfully running in production. Victoria confirms that she will be keeping the team together to work on the next release. The two stakeholders are relieved to hear this, and not only acquiesce to waiting until the next iteration for their desired functionality but offer to be involved with any requirements elicitation sessions. The demo is a success and everyone is excited to hear that the deployment into production is planned to occur two weeks from now.

**The retrospective.** The team is very excited to be this close to releasing their solution in production. Several people on the team believe that the Transition phase is going to go very smoothly given the quality of the work that they've done.

Terry shares the updated release burnup chart with the team. Terry compliments the team for both hitting the desired date and for implementing all of the "must have" functionality identified for this release by the stakeholders. He says that there is clearly more work to do next iteration and fully expects that the team will receive more requirements given the positive response in the demo earlier today.

Both Danny and Ashok point out how they're looking forward to a bit of a break as they're a bit worn out from having to consistently deliver a consumable solution every two weeks. Carlos agrees, pointing out that its common for agile teams to slowly burn themselves out if they don't pay attention to working at a sustainable pace throughout Construction. Carlos thinks that this is something the team should work at during the next release and the rest of the team agrees.

Tara brings up the problem she ran into with pre-production integration testing. In hindsight she feels that it was left too late in the lifecycle, although doesn't see how it could have been done earlier given her lack of access to the appropriate environment. Carlos describes a disciplined agile practice called parallel independent testing where the development team still tests to the best of its ability but also provides their working build on a regular basis to an independent test team. This team takes their build, and the builds from other teams developing other solutions, and integrates it into a pre-production testing environment (sometimes called a "QA environment" in traditional organizations). The test team then performs the kind of testing that the development team isn't likely to be able to perform, and reports any potential issues back to the appropriate development team(s). Carlos believes that this will help the team to avoid the "hardening sprint" anti-pattern in future releases.

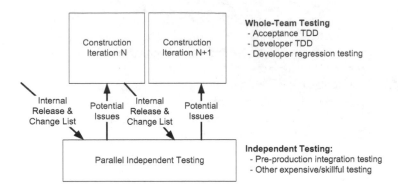

**The *Sufficient Functionality* milestone review.** Terry and Patricia meet with Padma the PMO lead, Berhard, and Victoria to hold a milestone review. Terry has pushed to keep this as light-weight as possible. Terry summarizes the current status of the team, walking everyone through the burnup chart and the defect trend chart. Patricia and Berhard summarize the results of the demo earlier in the day for Padma, who hadn't been able to attend. After a brief discussion everyone agrees that the Sufficient *Functionality* milestone has been passed successfully.

# 11 TRANSITION

The focus of the Transition phase in the Disciplined Agile Delivery (DAD) framework is for a team to release their consumable solution into production successfully. This should be done in as lightweight a manner as possible. As you can see there are two process goals to address during Transition, first to ensure that you're ready to deploy and second to actually deploy.

**Transition Goals**

**Ensuring that the solution is ready to deploy**. To do this, the team needs to:

- **Perform final testing and fixing**. The final testing effort is very short, at least by BigBank standards, due to the number of automated regression tests and due to the hardening work during Iteration C10. Tara, Danny, and Dick spend a lot of time testing in the pre-production environment, writing up a brief defect report for each potential issue they found. The issues are prioritized by Patricia as severity one through four. Any severity one defects have to be fixed, severity two defects should be fixed, and threes and fours are left to a future release if need be. These defects are tracked in Tara's spreadsheet and the defect trend report presented in the daily coordination meeting. It is common for Berhard and someone from Oliver's operations team to attend these coordination meetings.
- **Support training of the help desk staff**. Training is delivered to Samira's help desk team over a period of six days. Each training session took three hours to run and was presented to a portion of the help desk staff each time. During each training session either Ashok or Terry attends so as to answer any specific questions participants have about MAP.
- **Finalize the deliverable documentation**. This proves to

be a very minor effort due to the continuous documentation work performed by the team during Construction. Final reviews of the documentation are held with key stakeholders of each document, and appropriate changes are made. For the most part the reviewers find minor consistency problems with the documents, a common problem when documentation is evolved over time (people sometimes forget to go back and update previously written material).

- **Support development of end-user training videos**. The team is asked to help record seven two-minute training videos to be delivered as part of the overall solution. There is a brief overview of MAP and six "how to" instructional videos. Debbie, Patricia, and Barbara work together with Mary-Jane to finalize the scripts. Mary-Jane hires a professional actor to record the videos.

- **Validate the deployment scripts**. Ashok and Tara work with Oswald, an operations engineer from Oliver's team, to review and validate the deployment scripts. Tara has already thoroughly tested these scripts in the pre-production environment, in fact she has been using them for several weeks successfully. The scripts are written so that environment information, such as the names and IP addresses of machines, are maintained in configuration files. As a result the review just needs to focus on the contents of the configuration file describing the production environment.

**Deploying the solution**. Oswald runs the deployment scripts to release the solution into production. Due to regulatory compliance needs, BigBank has a strict policy of separating the development roles and release management roles. In effect someone who is actively involved with development is not allowed to deploy into production. Instead someone from Oliver's team must perform this work. This is why Oswald, and not a team member, is responsible for running the deployment scripts. It takes less than ten minutes to do so.

**Preparing for the next release**. During some free time the team meets for one hour to do initial release planning for the next release. This release took about six calendar months – three weeks for Inception, twenty for Construction, and two for Transition –

but at the prodding of Berhard the team decides that the next release should take only four months. Patricia holds some requirements envisioning sessions to identify requirements for the following release. This comprises a two-hour requirements envisioning session with several key stakeholders, followed the next day by a one-hour prioritization meeting. This effectively gives the team a head start on Inception for the second release. Unfortunately the team doesn't have time to size the new requirements, so that work moves into a two-week "Inception phase" for release 2.

When you keep a team together so that they can work on the next release you find that the Inception effort becomes much less (the team is already together, the environments are set up, the architecture is in place, funding is usually in place, and so on). In fact, most of the remaining Inception effort focuses on scoping and planning the next release, and that's typically a short effort. In this team's case they are able to complete it during their spare time during Transition.

Although the average agile team spends about a month performing Transition activities, the Mortgage Application Portal (MAP) team is able to do it in only two weeks. They are able to do this because of their focus on quality and testing issues throughout Construction; their adoption of the continuous documentation practice; their practice of automatically deploying their working build into demo and test environments (a big step towards continuous deployment); and working closely with operations and support staff to plan their deployment. Furthermore, the team feels that it could have been one week had it not been for the need to spread out the training of the support staff. Next release they hope Transition will be faster as the MAP will not be a new system and they will require less training.

# 12 FURTHER RELEASES

Over the long term the Mortgage Application Portal (MAP) application proves to be a successful system for BigBank. The first release, which focuses on providing mortgage information for existing customers and information about mortgage options, is well accepted by BigBank customers. It results in a measurable decrease in support desk calls and information requests in branches for mortgage information, providing important cost savings to BigBank. The second release, which adds the ability for new and existing customers to begin the mortgage application process online, provides both a significant cost savings as well as a revenue increase through a greater renewal rate. Subsequent releases add new and more sophisticated offerings.

In this chapter we overview the team's process improvement journey. Over the span of several releases the team evolves from their initial, Scrum-based agile lifecycle to a lean lifecycle and then eventually to a continuous delivery lifecycle.

## Release 2

Release two begins with a two-week Inception phase. During this period the team spends several hours sizing the new requirements that Patricia has identified the previous week. Debbie and Ashok each decide to take the first week off for vacation and Dick takes off both Fridays so that he can have two long weekends. The team also takes a three-day introductory course in test-driven development (TDD) the second week as this is a practice that has intrigued several team members ever since they started regression testing within the team during release one. This phase also overlaps with the warranty period for release one where the team had to be available to fix any production problems. During the first week of Inception a few severity two and severity three issues are identified and fixed. A patch is deployed into production, once again working with Oswald, over the weekend.

The Construction phase consists of seven two-week iterations. Here are the highlights of what happens:

- **TDD**. The team's adoption of TDD is a bit rough at first but goes well over time. Carlos spends a lot of time coaching team members in TDD, pairing with each team member an hour a day for the first three iterations. Tara also spends similar amounts of time pairing with people to help them gain basic unit testing skills. By the end of the release everyone is comfortable with taking a test-driven approach although felt that they still need to work on growing their skills. Team members with good design skills to start with find it much easier to pick up TDD then those without such skills.

- **Working from home**. Before agile was introduced into BigBank it was common for people to work one or two days a week from home. The Scrum coaches that BigBank hired insisted on co-located teams, which from the point of view of reducing overall risk is a great idea. However, from the point of view of the people who are used to working from home sometimes it is a great inconvenience. During Iteration C2 Carlos, the DAD coach, suggests that now that the team has gelled the team can safely experiment with letting people work from home occasionally. After discussing it with the team, Danny and Ashok begin to work from home one day a week. During Iteration C4 Debbie also starts to work at home one day a week. To support dispersed team members two tools are adopted, Atlassian's JIRA and HipChat. JIRA enables the team to manage their work item list and task board and will generate critical management reports including the iteration burndown and the release burnup charts. HipChat, as its name implies, is a chat system that integrates with JIRA. HipChat also supports videoconferencing, a feature that team members frequently use for collaborating whenever someone is working from home.

- **Improvement tracking**. During Iteration C1's retrospective Carlos suggests that the team begins to measure their improvement efforts. He describes a DAD technique called measured improvement where at each retrospective the team rates how well they are doing at addressing the previously identified improvements. The way that they do this is that they go through the list one at a time and each person is asked to rate, on a scale of one to ten, how well they think the team is doing. The votes are captured in a spreadsheet so that the trends can be publicly displayed in the team room as one of the information radiators. If an improvement starts to trend downward that's an indication that the team needs to refocus on that improvement. When an improvement levels off for many iterations, that's an indication that the team has either plateaued and may need to consider another strategy or that it has adopted the improvement as best it is going to and doesn't need to focus on it any longer.

- **The team evolves**. The team interviews several potential candidates to join the team and brings on David, a developer who is new to BigBank, the second week of Iteration C3. At the start of Iteration C5 Doug, an existing BigBank employee, joins the team after being interviewed by the team. Because collaboration and teamwork are so important to agile teams, they need to take responsibility for determining who will join them. Their personnel department, or "human resources" department in many cases, can often narrow down the number of likely candidates for the team to consider. However, the team itself should make the final decision as to who becomes a member, not a manager who is external to the team. Doug is joining the team because Debbie is rotating onto another team. While the team has grown to become extremely efficient and intends to stay together long-term, it is a good idea to rotate team members to keep them stimulated and to give them new learning opportunities.

- **Parallel independent testing**. As Carlos suggested towards the end of release one the team works with BigBank's quality assurance (QA) team to have them begin testing new MAP builds in parallel to their development efforts. Negotiations to do this began in Iteration C1 but it takes almost two months for the QA team to make the right people, Thomas and Tatiana, available to do this testing. The challenge is finding people with sufficient skills to do this work. Many of the testers on the QA team are "old school" and need to work from a detailed requirements specification. That isn't going to work for agile parallel independent testing because it is unlikely that there is going to be such a specification. Nor is it likely that the team is going to take on the overhead of doing so simply to support this type of testing, and that was certainly the case with MAP. Instead people with a more sophisticated testing skillset are needed, particularly around exploratory testing and end-to-end cross system integration testing. Carlos needs to work with Quincy, the QA manager, to educate him on how agile teams work and on the implications for his team. All of this takes time, and it isn't until the end of Iteration 4 that parallel independent testing begins. To report potential issues back to the team Thomas and Tatiana captured them using HP Quality Center which everyone in the QA team uses. Ideally they want to use JIRA but Quincy wouldn't support that. In the end Tara and Patricia needs to review the reported issues, Tara captures them in JIRA so that the team can easily access them, and Patricia prioritizes them so that the issue is treated as another type of requirement. Quincy is surprised by how few defects were found by the independent testing team. Carlos explains that due to the greater focus of all team members on quality and testing each other's work during the iteration that good agile teams doesn't let many defects "escape" the iteration. For agile teams, done means done – built and tested.

- **Vacations**. Danny takes two weeks off for vacation during Iteration C4 and Terry takes one week during Iteration C6. Members of agile teams, just like members of other teams, get to take vacation time. When they are gone the team's capacity to perform work is correspondingly lower, something that is taken into account during iteration planning.

The Transition phase takes one week this release, down from two weeks the previous release. This is the result of the need for less training required for the support staff and better overall quality due to improved testing during Construction. Additionally, the team benefits from their investment in automated deployment scripting and testing in the prior release. The training sessions were one hour each, compared with three hours each during the first release, allowing the team to schedule all of the training sessions on a single day. The team's approach to testing, in particular the adoption of TDD and parallel independent testing, dramatically reduces the need for hardening. However, there is still some hardening required, something that Carlos hopes to coach the team about next release.

## Release 3

Release 3 is shortened to three months, with one week for Inception, six two-week Construction iterations, and one week for Transition. The following events of interest occurred this release:

- **Training**. During Inception the team attends a two-day training workshop in acceptance test-driven development (ATDD), also called behavior driven development (BDD). After their experiences with unit/design-level TDD during release two, team members feel that they should take the next step and start trying TDD at the requirements level.

- **Requirements envisioning.** Patricia runs a half-day requirements elicitation workshop with a group of stakeholders to flesh out new requirements. This occurs on the second day of the Inception phase and the session is attended by all team members so that they can hear directly what the stakeholders wanted.

- **Improved quality**. A few minor issues, all severity three or four, are found during the warranty period following the second release. These issues are prioritized and added to the team's work item list. Victoria, the VP of IT at BigBank, publicly commends the MAP team in one of her monthly newsletters for their high quality and stakeholder satisfaction ratings that they were consistently receiving.

- **Continuous deployment**. Although the team started to automate their deployment during the first release, it wasn't until now that it became truly continuous. By the end of Release 3 the team has set up deployment so that successful builds are automatically promoted from someone's workstation to their team integration environment, and from the team integration environment into their demo environment and a staging environment for the independent test team. Using feature toggles, the team starts to "turn on" smaller pieces of functionality on a more frequent basis so they can do more frequent deployments to production. By architecting these small changes as isolated micro-services, the stakeholders felt more comfortable deploying these changes without large regression testing efforts.

- **Adoption of ATDD**. After their training the team actively started to adopt ATDD tooling and techniques. Tara invested about half of her time during the first three iterations pairing with Barbara, Doug, and Danny helping them to gain solid ATTD skills.

**Short Transition phase**. Transition is once again one week, although this was mostly because several team members decide to take vacation days. Inception for release #4 is performed in parallel.

## Releases 4+

The team continues improving the way that they work over time. The following key events occurred:

- **The release cadence was tightened**. To support Berhard's desire to shorten time to market, and to reduce overall risk on the MAP endeavor, the team actively tightens their release cadence over time: Release 4 was three months in length; Release 5 and 6 were both two months; and for Release 7 and beyond they settle on releasing every four weeks.
- **The lifecycle evolves**. As the result of discussions during several retrospectives during Release 5, the team decides to begin moving towards following DAD's Lean lifecycle. This is viable because the team has relatively easy access to stakeholders and because the team has gelled so well. At the beginning of Release 6 they choose to drop the concept of working in two-week iterations in favor of a continuous stream of development. Their first improvements are to hold weekly planning sessions and demos and hold retrospectives whenever someone on the team decides to call one (because they have an issue to discuss). During Release 8 the team replaces the weekly planning session in favor of replenishment sessions and

pull one work item at a time into their process (instead of a week's worth of work). The team is now capable of taking a new feature from the backlog and quickly building and deploying it to customers. This short cycle-time reduces work in process and provides a quick return on investment. With the team building, fixing, and deploying their own work they have in effect adopted the DevOps practice of "you build it, you run it" mentality. Carlos points out that the team had successfully evolved into DAD's Continuous Delivery lifecycle which is the most advanced and effective delivery lifecycle.

- **The team stops sizing.** Part of the decision to settle on a one-month release cadence is to provide a consistent and predictable schedule to stakeholders. This enables the team to convince their stakeholders to allow them to adopt a #NoEstimates[10] strategy where the team no longer takes on the overhead of sizing their work.

## BigBank's Overall Agile Transformation

The experiment with DAD on the MAP team is clearly a success. This is due to:

- BigBank's willingness to invest in training and coaching the team in disciplined agile techniques
- The team's willingness to learn together to adopt the agile mindset
- The team's willingness to try non-solo work techniques such as pair programming and agile modeling which enabled them to learn new skills faster
- Team members had good technical skills initially and were willing to expand those skills as needed

In parallel two other teams are also successful with DAD, prompting BigBank to start adopting it across many development teams. This occurs while the MAP team was in the middle of Release 2. A year later BigBank now has fifteen teams following a DAD-based approach and is looking to expand further.

---

[10] See http://noestimates.org/blog/

Carlos meets with senior executives from both the business and IT side of BigBank to explain that in order to obtain and sustain the maximum benefits of DAD they need to work on some transformational aspects as well. There are many organizational impediments at BigBank that need to be addressed over time to "grease the skids" for the agile teams. The executives agree to bring in a DAD Enterprise Coach to facilitate these changes. Using DAD's Exploratory/Lean Startup lifecycle for lean change management and the guidance provided in DAD 2.0 the Enterprise Coach works with BigBank to address IT-level activities such as Portfolio Management, Enterprise Architecture, DevOps, Data Management, and others as described in the appendix. Their experiences doing this will be described in detail in a forthcoming book tentatively titled *The Disciplined Agile IT Department*.

# 13 CLOSING THOUGHTS

We'd like to leave you with a few ideas around why you should consider adopting DAD, where you can learn more about DAD, and how you can get some help becoming more disciplined in your approach to agile solution delivery.

## Why DAD?

You should consider adopting the Disciplined Agile Delivery (DAD) framework when:

- You want a flexible and pragmatic agile framework rather than a purist agile method
- You are successfully using Scrum or Scrum/XP and want to take it to the next level
- You are using agile but have not been getting the results that you expected
- You are out of compliance with your PMO and want to incorporate some lightweight agile governance
- You are using Scrum but are unsure how to scale up
- You are using Scrum and are unsure how to address fundamental activities such architecture, testing, and analysis
- You have looked at SAFe but it appears to be too expensive and risky for your organization
- Your organization has adopted SAFe but run aground because you didn't have a solid foundation in place for your agile delivery teams
- You need to support several approaches to agile/lean development within your organization
- You need to understand how to effectively blend agile/lean initiatives with your projects that use a traditional approach

## How to Learn More

- As DAD continues to evolve, the latest material can be found at DisciplinedAgileDelivery.com. Signing up to follow the blog ensures that you receive updates when they are available.
- The certification program is maintained by the Disciplined Agile Consortium as described at DisciplinedAgileConsoritum.org
- Scott Ambler + Associates conducts a number of workshops on DAD. Whether you are new to agile/lean or experienced and want to take your capability to the next level, these workshops will start your journey. Detailed descriptions of courses and services can be found at ScottAmbler.com
- For other instructors of DAD workshops, a list of DAD Certified Instructors can be found at DisciplinedAgileConsortium.org/instructors

## Need Help?

Scott and Mark work with a team of seasoned enterprise and agile team coaches at Scott Ambler + Associates. Essentially, when we ask our clients "Why did you call us?" the common theme is that they have serious issues to deal with and need someone who knows how to solve the hard problems. They typically are either interested in moving from traditional approaches to agile or lean, or they have already tried but are not getting the benefits that they expected. Whether it be training, project coaching, or enterprise agile transformations, we can help.

For more information contact us at info@scottambler.com

# APPENDIX: THE DISCIPLINED AGILE IT DEPARTMENT

A disciplined agile IT department is a flexible learning organization that is responsive to the needs of the organization(s) that it supports and is able to do so in a financially effective manner.

First, some history about the focus of the Disciplined Agile (DA) process decision framework. Version 0.x, developed by IBM Rational under the leadership of Scott Ambler, between 2009 and the Autumn of 2011, was focused on agile software development. It was based on the observation that every team is unique and working in unique ways, and their efforts could be enhanced with flexible, light-weight process guidance. DA 1.x, developed between Autumn 2010 and the Spring of 2015 under the leadership of Scott Ambler and Mark Lines, was focused on a flexible, lightweight approach to IT solution delivery called Disciplined Agile Delivery (DAD). DA 1.0 is officially described in the book Disciplined Agile Delivery: A Practitioner's Guide to Agile Software Delivery in the Enterprise written by Scott and Mark and published by IBM Press in June 2012. Extensions and improvements to the framework were subsequently published at DisciplinedAgileDelivery.com. In June 2014 IBM officially recognized The Disciplined Agile Consortium (DisciplinedAgileConsortium.org) as the official source of all things DAD.

## Disciplined Agile IT

DA 2.x, extends disciplined agile strategies to the entire IT department. The development of DA 2.x began in the Spring of 2014 under the leadership of Scott and Mark. DA 2.x is based on several important observations. First, every organization is unique, and every IT department within each organization is also unique. Second, IT departments are dynamic complex adaptive systems that evolve over time. Third, the components of IT departments, teams and sub-departments, also evolve over time. Fourth, these components, when left to their own devices, are often not well aligned with each other or the enterprise. Worse yet, these groups may be working under their own locally optimized "improvement strategies." This misalignment is caused by competing leadership visions (or less delicately, by "politics") and exacerbated by disparate bodies of knowledge (BoKs) within our industry:

- The Agile cannon, disparate on its own, based on the Agile Manifesto, agilemanifesto.org.
- The Project Management Institute's BoK, pmi.org/PMBOK-Guide-and-Standards.aspx
- The Data Management BoK, dama.org/content/body-knowledge
- The Business Analysis BoK, iiba.org/babok-guide.aspx
- The Open Group Architecture Framework (TOGAF), opengroup.org/togaf/
- The Information Technology Infrastructure Library (ITIL), axelos.com/best-practice-solutions/itil
- The Control Objectives for Information and Related Technology (COBIT) framework, isaca.org/COBIT/Pages/default.aspx
- And many more

Although all of these bodies of work provide valuable insight, they each provide their own locally optimized view of how things should work. These views overlap, they provide inconsistent advice, and they are often focused on a single specialty. For example, the BA-BoK provides a business analyst-centric view, TOGAF provides an architecture centric view, the DM-BoK provides a data management centric view, and so on. All great views, but when combined with one another, which is a common approach in most organizations today looking for "best practices", they prove to be an ineffective mishmash. DA 2.x provides a coherent, integrated, high-level view of how an IT department may address all of these key areas in a consistent, flexible, and evolutionary manner. Wherever possible DA 2.x references the effective ideas in these BoKs and supplements them with strategies that are more consistent with modern agile approaches. The DA 2.0 framework is overviewed in the following diagram.

## Disciplined Agile 2.0

| | |
|---|---|
| **Disciplined Agile Delivery** Software teams follow a context-driven lifecycle | Continuous Delivery |
| | Exploratory/Lean Startup |
| | Lean/Advanced |
| | Agile/Basic |
| | Program Management |
| **Disciplined DevOps** Streamlined IT delivery and operations. | Non-Agile/Lean Lifecycles |
| | Release Management |
| | Operations |
| | Support |
| | Data Management |
| **Disciplined Agile IT** Everyone within the IT eco-system works in a collaborative, learning-oriented, evolutionary manner. | People Management |
| | Product Management |
| | Portfolio Management |
| | Enterprise Architecture |
| | Reuse Engineering |
| | IT Governance |
| | Continuous Improvement |

v2.1

Here is what's in the DA 2.x framework:

1. **Complete support for what has come before**. DA 2.x fully encompasses DA 1.x, extending it to fully support IT. One extension is the explicit addition of program management to address how large agile/lean teams are organized.

2. **Introduction of process blades**. DA 2.x has been arranged into components called "process blades." Each process blade focuses on a major IT activity, as you can see in the previous diagram. No blade is an island unto itself – each one is involved in workflows with several other blades. The implication is that a change in one area, such as a process improvement or a change in the organizational structure of the people involved, will potentially affect the instantiation of the other blades. This interconnection of processes and organization strategies is a reflection of the fact that IT departments are complex adaptive systems.

3. **Disciplined DevOps**. This is the streamlining of IT solution development and IT operations activities, and supporting enterprise-IT activities, to provide more effective outcomes to an organization. This extends Disciplined Agile Delivery to include non-agile/lean approaches to IT delivery (most IT departments have to support older ways of working in addition to agile/lean), release management, operations, support (help desk), and data management.

4. **Disciplined IT**. This portion of the framework includes process blades that cross the entire IT function. This includes people management (sometimes called human resources or talent management), product management, portfolio management, enterprise architecture, reuse engineering, IT governance, and continuous improvement.

## The Disciplined Agile 2.0 Process Blades

The process blades are:

- **Agile/Basic**. Describes the end-to-end solution delivery lifecycle for teams working in an agile, or Scrum-based, manner. Project teams who are new to agile, or who find themselves in situations where a regular work cadence is effective for them, will often choose to adopt this lifecycle.

- **Continuous Delivery**. Describes the end-to-end solution delivery lifecycle for teams working in a continuous delivery manner. Product teams who are working in a DevOps environment often adopt this strategy.

- **Continuous Improvement**. Addresses how to support process and organizational structure improvement across teams in a lightweight, collaborative manner; how to support improvement experiments within teams; and how to govern process improvement with the IT department.

- **Data Management**. Addresses how to improve data quality, evolve data assets such as master data and test data, and govern data activities within the organization.

- **Enterprise Architecture**. Addresses strategies for supporting stakeholders; supporting delivery teams; resolving technical dependencies between solutions; evolving the enterprise architecture; capturing the enterprise architecture; and governing the enterprise architecture efforts. For examples of a DA 2.0 goal diagram, please see the one for the Enterprise Architecture process blade on the following page and the one for Portfolio Management two pages later.

- **Exploratory/Lean Startup**. Describes the end-to-end solution delivery lifecycle for teams working in an exploratory, or "lean start up", manner. Teams who find themselves in situations where rapid innovation is called for often follow this lifecycle.

- **IT Governance**. Addresses strategies for consolidating various governance views, defining metrics, taking measurements, monitoring and reporting on measurements, developing and capturing guidance, defining roles and responsibilities, sharing knowledge within the organization, managing IT risk, and coordinating the various governance efforts (including EA governance).

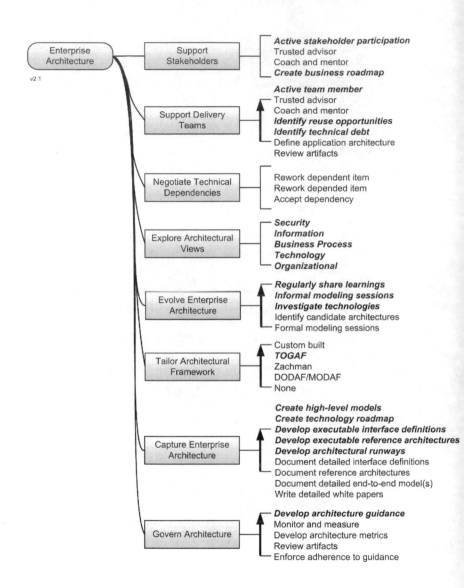

- **Lean/Advanced**. Describes the end-to-end solution delivery lifecycle for teams working in a lean, or Kanban-based, manner. Teams who have many small, relatively independent requirements (be they change requests or potential defects) and who are working on an existing solution will often adopt this lifecycle.
- **Operations**. Addresses how to run systems, evolve the IT infrastructure, manage change within the operational ecosystem, mitigate disasters, and govern IT operations.
- **Portfolio Management**. Addresses how to identify potential business value that could be supported by IT endeavors, explore those potential endeavors to understand them in greater detail, prioritize those potential endeavors, initiate the endeavors, manage vendors, and govern the IT portfolio.
- **Product Management**. Addresses strategies for managing a product, including allocating features to a product, evolving the business vision for a product, managing functional dependencies, and marketing the product line.
- **Program Management**. Addresses strategies for managing large product/project teams, allocating requirements between sub teams, managing dependencies between sub teams, coordinating the sub teams (via common or disparate cadences), and governing a program.
- **Release Management**. Addresses strategies for planning the IT release schedule, coordinating releases of solutions (such as release trains or release windows), managing the release infrastructure, supporting delivery teams, and governing the release management efforts.
- **Reuse Management**. Addresses how to identify and obtain reusable assets, publish the assets so that they are available to be reused, support delivery teams in reusing the assets, evolving those assets over time, and governing the reuse efforts.
- **Support**. Addresses how to adopt an IT support strategy, to escalate incidents, to effectively address the incidents, and govern the IT support effort.

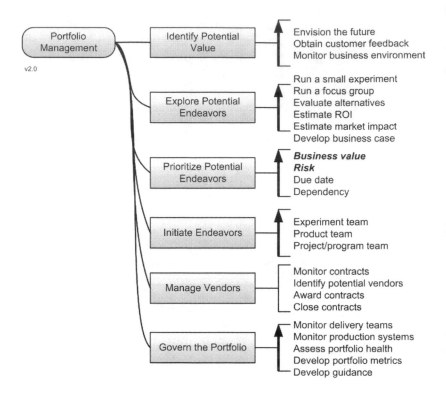

## Why Disciplined Agile IT?

The business environment is only becoming more competitive over time, with small nimble organizations competing in international marketplaces with large established competitors. This puts increasing pressure on existing enterprises to respond swiftly and effectively. They only way they can do this is if they have nimble IT departments that are sufficiently responsive. To increase the challenge, IT departments must be able to react to the changing needs of their organization while at the same time keep the existing IT infrastructure running smoothly. The only way that they can do this is by taking a flexible, holistic approach to the business of IT – This is exactly what Disciplined Agile IT is all about.

## Where to Get More Information

There are three primary sources for information about Disciplined Agile IT:

1. **The DAD site**. We regularly publish blog postings and articles at DisciplinedAgileDelivery.com.
2. **The DAC site**. At DisciplinedAgileConsortium.org we have a variety of whitepapers, presentations, recordings, and posters available for free download.
3. **LinkedIn**. There is a Disciplined Agile Delivery (DAD) discussion forum that is quite active.
4. **Our next book**. Our forthcoming book is tentatively titled *The Disciplined Agile IT Department*. We plan on releasing it during Q1 2016.

The Disciplined Agile Consortium (DAC) is actively investing in the evolution of the Disciplined Agile framework. We hope that you choose to get involved

# INDEX

## #

#NoEstimates, 85

## A

acceptance TDD, 83
Agile Modeling, 10
agile/basic lifecycle, 92
architecture envisioning, 34
architecture handbook, 36
architecture modeling
    technology roadmap, 57
automated deployment, 68

## B

backlog grooming, 52
basic/agile lifecycle, 17
BDD, 83
burnup chart, 64

## C

certification, 6, 88
coaching, 33, 85
COBIT, 90
collocation, 41
commitments, 48
consumable solutions, 25
context sensitive, 19, 25
continuous delivery lifecycle, 18,
    85, 93
continuous development, 84
continuous improvement, 93
continuous integration, 7, 18, 54,
68
coordination meeting, 46, 54

## D

DAD blog, 88
DAMA, 90
dashboard, 68
data management, 93
data modeling, 35, 49, 65
defect mgmt, 71, 75, 82
defect trend chart, 71
definition of done, 47
demo, 50, 56, 72
deployment planning, 69, 71
deployment testing, 76
development environment, 42
development intelligence, 69
DevOps, 23, 92
    you run it, 85
documentation, 64
    continuous, 65, 69, 76
    deliverable, 76
dropping scope, 49

## E

enterprise architecture, 23, 34,
    93
enterprise awareness, 23
exploratory lifecycle, 18
exploratory lifecycle, 93
Extreme Programming, 10

## F

fail fast, 25

feature toggles, 34

## G

Gantt chart, 40
goal diagram
  develop the initial release
    plan, 40
  explore initial scope, 20
  produce a potentially
    consumable solution, 58
goal driven
  Inception phase, 31
  mind map, 21
goal-driven, 19
governance, 8, 10, 23, 25, 87, 93

## H

hardening, 50, 55, 63, 83
history of DAD, 89
hybrid, 12

## I

IBM, 89
IIBA, 90
Inception phase, 31
IT governance, 93
iteration burndown, 48
iteration planning, 45, 53
iteration review, 50
ITIL, 90

## J

just in time design, 53

## K

Kanban, 10

## L

Lean Software Development, 10
lean/advanced lifecycle, 17, 84, 95
lifecycles, 12
look-ahead modeling, 53

## M

measured improvement, 80
micro-services, 34, 84
milestone
  delighted stakeholders, 40
  proven architecture, 56
  stakeholder vision, 44
  sufficient functionality, 64, 74
modeling
  data, 49
  initial architecture, 34
  initial requirements, 33
  just in time, 54
  look-ahead analysis, 52, 55, 61
  look-ahead design, 52
  upfront, 31
  usage, 33

## N

non-functional requirements, 36
non-solo work, 61

## O

operations, 95
Outside In Development, 10

## P

pairing, 61

parallel independent testing, 73, 82

planning
    date driven, 39
    deployment planning, 69, 71
    iteration planning, 45, 53
    release planning, 38, 69, 76
    scheduling, 40
    scope-driven, 39
planning poker, 37
PMI, 90
PMO, 44
portfolio management, 23, 95
pragmatic agile, 5
prioritization, 36, 77
process blades, 92
product management, 95
program management, 95
proof of concept, 37

## Q

quality assurance, 81

## R

refactoring
    legacy code, 35
regulatory compliance, 76
relative mass sizing, 38, 63
release management, 95
release planning, 38, 69, 76
requirements
    ATDD/BDD, 83
    envisioning, 33, 77, 83
retrospective, 51, 69, 73
    measured improvement, 80
reuse management, 95
risk management, 36
    delighted stakeholders, 40
    deployment risk, 35

mitigation of risk early, 37
proven architecture, 56
release cadence, 84
risk list, 42
stakeholder vision, 44
sufficient functionality, 64, 74
roles, 11

## S

scaling agile, 24
scaling factors, 25
scope creep, 61
screen sketches, 55
Scrum, 10
spike, 37
stabilization, 50
stakeholders, 40
standup meeting. *See*
    coordination meeting
story map, 34
succeed early, 25
support, 95

## T

task board, 46
team kickoff, 31
team room, 41
technology roadmap, 35, 56
test often, 68
test-after programming, 58
test-driven development, 79
test-first programming, 58
testing
    deployment testing, 76
    final testing, 75
    parallel independent testing, 73
testless programming, 58
time to market, 84

TOGAF, 90
training, 20, 85
   end users, 76
   stakeholders in DAD, 67
   support staff, 69, 71, 75
Transition phase, 75
transparency, 49

## U

Unified Process, 10
upfront planning, 7, 38
user stories, 45

## V

vacations, 82
velocity, 39, 56
vision statement, 43

## W

warranty period, 79
WaterScrumFall, 7
working from home, 80

# ABOUT THE AUTHORS

Scott W. Ambler is the Senior Consulting Partner of Scott Ambler + Associates, working with organizations around the world to help them improve their software processes. He provides training, coaching, and mentoring in disciplined agile and lean strategies at both the project and organization level. Scott is the founder of the *Agile Modeling (AM), Agile Data (AD), Disciplined Agile Delivery (DAD)*, and *Enterprise Unified Process (EUP) methodologies.* He is the (co-)author of several books, including *Disciplined Agile Delivery, Refactoring Databases, Agile Modeling, Agile Database Techniques, The Object Primer 3rd Edition*, and *The Enterprise Unified Process.* Scott blogs about DAD at DisciplinedAgileDelivery.com. Scott is also a *Founding Member of the Disciplined Agile Consortium (DAC)*, the certification body for disciplined agile.

Mark Lines is Managing Partner at Scott Ambler + Associates. He is an Enterprise Agile Coach and co-creator of the Disciplined Agile Delivery framework. Mark is co-author with Scott Ambler of *Disciplined Agile Delivery: A Practitioner's Guide to Agile Software Delivery in the Enterprise.* Mark helps organizations all over the world transform from traditional to disciplined agile and lean methods. He writes for many publications including the *Cutter Consortium* and is a frequent speaker at industry conferences. Mark blogs about DAD at DisciplinedAgileDelivery.com. He is also a founding member of the *Disciplined Agile Consortium (DAC)*, the certification body for disciplined agile.

43892060R00059

Made in the USA
Charleston, SC
07 July 2015